Singapore

Singapore

Text by J. D. Brown and Margaret Backenheimer
Edited by Dial House Publishing Ltd
Photography: Jon Davison, except pages 10, 18, 33, 38, 44, 49, 51, 61, 63, 64, 66, 69, 74, 85, 106, and 108: J. D. Brown
Cover photograph by Jon Davison
Cartography by Raffaele De Gennaro

Third Edition 2002

NO part of this book may be reproduced, stored in a retrieval system or transmitted in any form or means electronic, mechanical, photocopying, recording or otherwise, without prior written permission from Apa Publications. Brief text quotations with use of photographs are exempted for book review purposes only.

CONTACTING THE EDITORS
Every effort has been made to provide accurate information in this publication, but changes are inevitable. The publisher cannot be responsible for any resulting loss, inconvenience or injury. We would appreciate it if readers would call our attention to any errors or outdated information by contacting Berlitz Publishing, PO Box 7910, London SE1 1WE, England. Fax: (44) 20 7403 0290;
e-mail: berlitz@apaguide.demon.co.uk

All Rights Reserved

© 2002 Apa Publications GmbH & Co. Verlag KG, Singapore Branch, Singapore

Printed in Singapore by Insight Print Services (Pte) Ltd, 38 Joo Koon Road, Singapore 628990. Tel: (65) 6865-1600. Fax: (65) 6861-6438

Berlitz Trademark Reg. U.S. Patent Office and other countries. Marca Registrada. Used under licence from the Berlitz Investment Corporation

060/203 REV.

CONTENTS

Singapore and its People	7

A Brief History	14

Where to Go	24
Singapore River	24
The Civic District	32
Chinatown	41
Little India	47
Kampong Glam	50
Orchard Road	54
Geylang Serai	57
Zoos, Parks, and Orchids	58
Island Excursions	68

What to Do	77
Shopping	77
Entertainment	84
Sports	88
Singapore for Children	91
Festivals and Events	93

Eating Out	96

Handy Travel Tips	109

Hotels and Restaurants	131

Index	143

● A ☛ in the text denotes a highly recommended sight

Singapore

SINGAPORE AND ITS PEOPLE

Singapore is a very small island nation with very large attractions and achievements. Strategically situated on the tip of the Malaysian peninsula between the Indian Ocean and the South China Sea, Singapore has made itself the busiest port in the world, the second largest oil refiner on the planet, and a major international financial center. While Singapore's astonishing wealth sets it apart from most tiny islands, it is its population that makes it unique. A melding of Chinese, Malay, and Indian peoples, this Southeast-Asian crossroads has become a model of ethnic and religious harmony. Singapore also stands out as the cleanest, most efficient, most highly organized society in Asia.

Yet what attracts travelers is not Singapore's wealth or its social wisdom; it is the shopping, the eating, and the ethnic neighborhoods of the island. Shopping and eating are the chief activities of the Singaporeans themselves, and it isn't long before visitors are swept up in these tides of delightful consumerism. Because of its special location and status as a free-trade zone, Singapore boasts good shopping for clothing, crafts, jewelry, and goods manufactured in nearby Bali, Malaysia, Thailand, and other handicraft centers of southeast Asia.

> In Singapore, respect is shown to one's elders; by law, children must support their parents in retirement years.

Again, because of its location, Singapore offers the most diverse culinary experience of any Asian nation. Here, the very best Chinese, Indian, Malaysian, and Indonesian dishes are readily available, routinely at rock-bottom prices.

Singaporean children out for a history lesson.

Finally, for the sightseer and cultural explorer, Singapore offers historic districts to explore, from Arab Street and Little India to the Colonial District and a sprawling Chinatown. There are world-class modern attractions as well, from orchid gardens to one of the world's finest zoos. These treasures are themselves tiny but brilliant isles in an urban sea of modern shopping malls (one with the world's largest fountain), government housing towers (home to millions of residents), and skyscrapers (where all the money is counted).

It is curious how so much (culturally, ethnically, and economically) is contained in so small a space. The main island of Singapore, together with over 60 surrounding islets, covers about 250 square miles (660 sq km) — four times smaller than Luxembourg or Rhode Island (the smallest state in the US). Yet about half of this land consists of forest reserves, marshes, and other green areas.

Singapore's green zones surprise many first-time visitors, at least those expecting to find a colossal air-conditioned city-state of glass and steel housed under a plastic bubble. While crowded and expanding, with a population approaching 4 million, Singapore is not the sprawling patchwork of overlapping suburbs and housing developments one

Singapore and its People

encounters in many large modern cities, such as Los Angeles. Instead, Singapore can be said to be a vertical Los Angeles. Upwards of 90 percent of its residents live in housing estates that consist of neatly kept apartment towers stretching to the sky. These residential towers are distributed across the main island in new towns, many of which have their own subway stations, shopping malls, libraries, recreational halls, and other urban services. Within the tower clusters, and between the towns, there are extensive green zones and areas of parkland.

Although linked to Malaysia by geography and by history, Singapore is an independent country, with a population dominated by the Chinese (76.8 percent). Malays make up 13.9 percent of Singapore's citizens, followed by Indians (7.9 percent). There are four official languages (English, Malay, Mandarin Chinese, and Tamil), with English designated as the language of administration and Malay as the national language. In fact, most Chinese people speak a

Worshippers offer incense to the Buddhist Goddess of Mercy at the Kuan Im Tong Hood Temple.

Singapore is a successful multi-ethnic society.

variety of languages, especially Hokkien, Teochew, and Cantonese, reflecting the various origins of the Singaporean Chinese.

One ethnic group that played a large part in shaping the customs, architecture, and cuisine of Singapore was the Straits Chinese or Peranakans, a hybrid race that evolved from intermarriage between Chinese migrants from mainland China and native Malays. The Peranakan subculture of *babas* (men) and *nonyas* (women) is a charming blend of Malay, Chinese, and British elements. The British themselves also exerted a lasting influence on the language, customs, and administration, since they literally created modern Singapore in 1819, and guided its destiny until a new self-governing constitution was approved in 1959.

Singapore is a well-wired nation. All homes are linked to a countrywide network of fiber-optic cables supplying a range of services, from cable TV (40 channels) to the internet. The government's goal is to connect the whole nation to one open network, known as Singapore ONE (One Network for Everyone).

In Singapore's highly efficient society, transportation is a showcase of national industry. The subway (MRT) serves over 1 million people daily, and continues to expand to all corners of the main island. The subway is quick and easy for foreigners to use. Over 18,000 taxis serve the city. Singapore's cabs are inexpensive and clean, and they accept a variety of credit cards. Only about a third of Singapore's residents (who enjoy the second highest per capita income in Asia) can afford a personal car, due to the deliberate imposition of high taxes, restrictions on car use, and tariffs levied on automobile ownership. This, along with other tough traffic regulations, has kept the downtown area from experiencing the gridlock and road rage common to other metro-

Singapore Tidbits

- Singapore's Keppel Harbor is the world's busiest port.
- Singapore supports more plant species than exist in all of North America.
- The most popular leisure activity among Singaporeans is watching TV.
- The best math students in the world attend Singapore schools.
- The Singapore Sling is still served at the place it was invented almost a century ago, the Long Bar in the Raffles Hotel.
- Nearly all (86%) of Singaporeans live in high-rise residential towers, most built by the government.
- The Suntec City mall contains the world's largest fountain.
- The lowest temperature ever recorded in Singapore was 68.9° F (19.4° C).
- Less than 60% of Singapore households have an air conditioner.
- The number of yearly visitors is twice the total population.

politan areas. Singapore's airport, often hailed as the best in the world, enjoys the same unrestricted flow; clearing customs and immigration is often a matter of how fast you can walk.

Of course, Singapore's efficiency, orderliness, cleanliness, and general good behavior has come at what some critics consider a steep price. Even locals joke that Singapore is a "fine" country, seeing as how the government has imposed a fine on nearly every objectionable behavior, from not flushing public toilets to selling chewing gum. Singapore is also known as a country with severe penalties for more serious offenses. Caning is still prescribed for some crimes; the death penalty is always enforced for drug smuggling. But what some Westerners perceive as an authoritarian city-state, with draconian laws and little personal freedom, is regarded by most Singaporeans as merely the common-sense way to run society. Singapore's economic success, and its ability to combat such social ills as drug use, corruption, and pollution, have made it the envy of many emerging nations and a model for Asia in general.

> Singapore's leading cartoon character, *Kiasu*, is a pushy, me-first, win-at-all-costs gentleman who rebels at the city's noted conformist mentality – and thus epitomizes for many the real "hate-to-lose" Singaporean.

For skeptical Westerners, seeing Singapore for themselves can be an eye-opener. This is certainly not an oppressed population. On the contrary, Singaporeans tend to be outgoing and cheerful, if a little competitive and aggressive. Some say that social engineering in Singapore has proved a success because it is built on the traditional Confucian and Asian values of the region. While Singapore is cosmopolitan, modern, very hard working, and Western in outlook, it is at core a

Singapore and its People

society of people who place a high value on family and nation, on racial tolerance and consensus.

While few visitors might judge the politics of Singapore as oppressive, everyone could be forgiven for finding the weather so. Just 80 miles (130 km) north of the equator, Singapore is hot and humid year-round. It hardly cools off at night by more than a few degrees. The lowest temperature ever recorded in Singapore was a "chilling" 68.9°F (19.4°C). The daily doses of high humidity leave most foreign visitors drenched in sweat shortly after hitting the streets. Fortunately, ever-ingenious Singapore has taken on the forces of the climate, too. In public areas, everything that can be air-conditioned usually is, from buses to big shopping malls and most cabs.

For some travelers, Singapore is a welcome stopover, an island of Western-style luxury with a top-rated airport which makes it the perfect gateway to Thailand, Indonesia (Bali and Java), Malaysia, Cambodia, and Vietnam. For others, Singapore, with its legendary cleanliness and hygiene, its widespread use of English, and its celebrated sights, shops, and ethnic eateries, is a significant destination in its own right – an ideal introduction, in fact, to all of Asia.

Hindu deities on the Sri Mariamman temple roof.

A BRIEF HISTORY

With its location at the crossroads of southeast Asia's sea-lanes, it's no surprise that Singapore has long functioned as a major trading post. Malay, Indian, and Chinese merchants plied the Straits of Malacca for centuries; Chinese sailors apparently named the island Pu-luo-chung (Island at Land's End) as early as the 3rd century A.D. Malays settled the isle by the 7th century, naming it Temasek (Sea Town), and Marco Polo may have sailed by it in the late 13th century. About 1299, a Sumatran prince, seeking shelter from a storm, gave the island its modern name after sighting what he thought was a lion — more likely a tiger, native to Singapore and Malaysia. Singapura is Sanskrit for Lion City, and Singapore has been the Lion City ever since, regardless of the fact that no wild lions ever roamed here.

Pirates used the island as a base for centuries, as control of Singapore, the Malaysian peninsula, and the Straits of Malacca wavered between Siamese and East Javan conquerors until the arrival of a man named Raffles, the founder of modern Singapore.

Raffles Rules

Sir Thomas Stamford Raffles (1781–1826) only visited Singapore briefly over a four-year period, but he left a giant's imprint on the island. An officer of the British East India Company and a colonial entrepreneur of extraordinary vision, Raffles spoke the Malay language and knew its customs. He governed Java, writing a history of the region, but his goal was to establish a trading post in strategic waters between Indonesia and Malaysia where the Dutch, as well as the British, had considerable colonial holdings. Raffles succeeded in this aim when he landed on the banks of the

Historical Landmarks

A.D. 100–300 Malay, Indian, and Chinese sailors ply the Straits of Singapore.

A.D. 600–700 Malays settle the island, naming it Temasek.

1292-1295 Marco Polo visits Malaysia's "Chiamassie" port, possibly Singapore.

1299 Singapore (Sanskrit for "Lion City') is named by a Sumatran prince.

1415 China's "Columbus," Cheng Ho, complains of pirates in the Singaporean isles.

1819 Sir Thomas Stamford Raffles makes Singapore a British trading post.

1820 Chinese immigrants arrive as laborers in Singapore.

1824 Singapore is purchased by the British East India Company.

1826 Singapore is administered by the East India Company as part of Straits Settlements.

1867 Singapore becomes a British colony.

1876 Rubber-tree plantations are planted in Malaysia.

1906 China's Sun Yat Sen visits Singapore to establish a revolutionary political party.

1942 Singapore is occupied by Japanese armies and renamed Syonan (Southern Light).

1945 Japan is ousted from Singapore.

1946 The British make Singapore a Crown Colony.

1955 David Marshall heads the first elected government.

1959 Lee Kuan Yew and the People's Action Party (PAP) control the new parliament.

1963 Singapore joins the new nation of Malaysia.

1965 Singapore is forced out of Malaysia and becomes an independent state. Lee Kuan Yew heads the new Republic of Singapore.

1969 The government bans trial by jury.

1990 Goh Chok Tong takes over from Lee Kuan Yew who continues to serve as powerful Senior Minister.

2002 Visitors top 7 million a year.

The Sir Stamford Raffles statue and landing place.

Singapore River on January 29, 1819, and signed treaties with contending Malay sultans, thus establishing Singapore as a British trading post. The Dutch recognized the claim in 1824. In 1831, Malacca, Penang, and Singapore effectively became British trading colonies under the British Straits Settlements.

Upon his arrival in 1819, Raffles found an island shrouded in dense jungle and swamp, occupied by a few Malay families and some Chinese traders. Free trade policies and firm but liberal colonial rule under Raffles' direction soon created a boomtown of 10,000 residents where 2,000 ships called annually. The sultans sold their rights to Singapore in 1824, and Raffles continued his social reforms (abolishing slavery), cleared the land, and oversaw an ambitious construction campaign. He opened Singapore to immigration, bringing in laborers, merchants, and businessmen from all over southeast Asia, most notably from China. Raffles, in short, laid the groundwork for the vibrant free port of Singapore that remains in place today.

Raffles created colonial Singapore in astonishingly short order. He stayed only a week on his first visit in 1819, placing Colonel William Farquhar in command. He returned the same year for three weeks, devising the familiar outlines of the city, with its Colonial District on the Singapore River. When Raffles next visited three years later, he relieved Farquhar of command and oversaw the final details of Singapore's reconstruction. By the time Raffles departed Singapore for the last time, in June 1823, he had laid the cornerstone for a college that united Malaysian and European students in East-West studies. The following year, a ship fire destroyed all his writings about the region and his extensive natural history specimens. He died without heir in London in 1826, a day short of his 45th birthday.

Rubber and Tin

The British success in Singapore depended on many elements, including cooperation with the Chinese clan organizations (the *kong si*) and complicity in the opium trade, which was a major source of revenue from the 1830s onwards. Singapore became a British colony officially in 1867, just before the opening of the Suez Canal, which further spurred trade in the Straits of Malacca. In the first

Chinatown shophouses, home to prosperous merchants.

Singapore

fifty years after Raffles' appearance, the island's population mushroomed from a few hundred to over 100,000. As the 20th century loomed, the export of Malaysian rubber and tin became Singapore's major industry. The pirate coves and tiger dens of earlier times were erased; rubber plantations and tin mines ruled the region.

Generations of Chinese born in Malaysia, many of whom married locals, came to be ardent supporters of British ways. These Straits Chinese dominated local politics and formed the wealthier ranks of the mercantile class under colonial rule, but they kept in touch with the Chinese mainland, as well. Sun Yat Sen arrived in Singapore to set up a branch of his revolutionary party in 1906. The Great Depression in the West swept through in 1929, hurling many miners and rubber tappers into extreme poverty, but the 1920s also saw the ascent of Singapore millionaires, including Aw Boon Haw, the purveyor of Tiger Balm. Discontent with colonial rule increased in the 1930s, with the rise of India's independence movement on one side and of China's Communist Party on the other, but revolution was put on hold by the approach of the Japanese armies, bent on Asia's conquest, and by the beginnings of the Second World War.

Traditional Chinese stories brought to life at Aw Boon Haw's Tiger Balm Gardens.

The Fall of Singapore

Winston Churchill would call the fall of Singapore to the advancing Japanese forces in 1942 "the worst disaster and the largest capitulation" in English history. Singaporeans, even today, certainly do not feel they were well protected by their colonial masters. The British, confident of an attack from the sea, had built a strong naval defense at Singapore and armed Sentosa Island to the south with large guns, but the Japanese came by land, sweeping down the Malaysian peninsula on foot and by bicycle, seizing nearby Johor Baru. Outnumbered three to one, the Japanese nevertheless struck quickly, occupying Bukit Timah, with its food and fuel depots, and bluffed the British into surrender seven days after landing on Singapore. Singapore fared poorly. Nearly 30,000 prisoners of war were incarcerated in Changi Prison, near Singapore's present airport. They were later led on a forced march through Malaysia all the way to Thailand, where many died building the railway and bridge over the River Kwai.

Standing on guard at Fort Canning.

Residents of Singapore, especially those of Chinese ancestry, were punished even more severely than the Australian, Indian, and British soldiers, since they had opposed Japan's earlier occupation of China. By the time of Japan's surrender in 1945, about 100,000 Singapore resi-

19

Last resting place: the Old Cemetery at Fort Canning.

dents had died through execution, or starvation.

The British resumed control after the Second World War, but their authority was much diminished and Singapore's desire for political autonomy was strong. The British gradually relaxed their control in the region, creating a Federation of Malaya for Malaysians and making Singapore, which was predominately Chinese, a separate Crown Colony in 1955. The colony's first chief minister, David Marshall, demanded independence, but Britain refused. Meanwhile, a new party was rising in Singapore, headed by a new leader who would shape a modern Singapore as profoundly as Raffles had shaped the colonial city-state.

Lee Kuan Yew in Charge

Singapore's modern-day Raffles was Lee Kuan Yew. Lee was born in 1923 to Straits Chinese parents, attended the college Raffles had established, and then graduated from Cambridge with honors. Returning to Singapore in 1950, he cast his lot with those advocating the overthrow of the British colonialists, helping form the People's Action Party (PAP) in 1955. Supporting labor unions, working with local communists, and calling for a merger with the rest of

History

Malaysia, the PAP won the first internal self-government elections of 1959 and Lee became Singapore's prime minister. Quickly severing his ties to communist and leftist elements, Lee concentrated on severing ties with Britain by uniting with Malaysia, Sabah and Sarawak to create the Federation of Malaysia, formed in 1963.

It was not long, however, before Singapore was being viewed as a political and ethnic threat to the new Malaysian republic. Muslim forces hastened the expulsion of Singapore, which came in 1965, dashing Lee's dream of Malaysian unity after just 23 months, but leading directly to Singapore's full independence.

Many doubted whether Singapore had the resources, the will, and the genius to survive as a tiny independent nation, but Lee seemed to supply all three elements. As prime minister from 1959 to 1990, Lee has been hailed, especially in Singapore itself, as the singular architect of his nation. He harmonized the contending ethnic forces in Singapore, brought strict order to society, emphasized efficiency, embraced Western ideas, dealt harshly with his political opponents, ruled the nation like a father, and focused unrelentingly on economic progress. So far, his People's

War Memorial Park: past memories and future hopes.

Action Party has not spent a single day out of office since independence, and most Singaporeans venerate Lee Kuan Yew as their founding father.

The New Singapore

Under Lee Kuan Yew and his successor, Goh Chok Tong, Singapore has continued to be one of Southeast Asia's brightest stars the last three decades. The paternal approach of the government has defused racial and labor disputes, government housing schemes have provided most citizens with their own homes, and trade and business policies have attracted plenty of foreign trade and investment. While the massive modernization of Singapore has its critics, and much of old Singapore has been razed, the standard of living has risen to the highest international standards. The government's social engineering projects — which include banning smoking in public places, outlawing the sale of chewing gum, monitoring public toilets for flushing, imposing huge taxes on automobile ownership, and running state-sponsored matchmaking services — have all drawn sneers from overseas, but Singapore is the most mannerly and clean of all Asian capitals (Tokyo included).

From the perspective of Western democracies, Singapore's great achievements have come at the expense of personal and political freedoms. Dissidents have been jailed or exiled, critical publications have been banned (*Asian Wall Street Journal*, 1985) or sued (*International Herald Tribune*, 1994) for unflattering coverage, and the local media, from TV to newspapers, have often censored themselves into blandness. The case of David Marshall (1908–1995), one of Singapore's founding fathers, is illustrative. A Singapore-born Jew whose parents were from Iraq, Marshall was educated in Britain, became a prisoner of war when the

Japanese invaded Singapore, and established himself as Singapore's best criminal defense attorney. He was elected as Singapore's first chief minister in 1955 but, with the rise of Lee Kuan Yew and the PAP, soon found himself cast in the role of dissenter. In 1969, Lee and his government banned all trials by jury, putting a severe dent in Marshall's high-profile career. Marshall was among the very few in Singapore to openly oppose caning as a punishment in minor criminal cases. The year before his death he branded Lee a fascist.

Singapore's name (which means Lion City) is symbolised by the Merlion.

Such a view in Singapore today is decidedly that of the minority. Full employment, bureaucratic efficiency, social stability, and a continued high standard of living have pleased most residents, who are free to vote out the ruling party under Singapore's parliamentary system. The ruling party has promised to open the political process to the people and, by making Singapore a more cultured society, stem the "brain drain" exodus of some of its most qualified and highly educated citizens to the West. How Singapore shapes itself to fit an era of raised expectations in the 21st century remains an open question, one that may take the rise of another Stamford Raffles or Lee Kuan Yew to answer.

Singapore

WHERE TO GO

Singapore can take days to explore. In addition to excellent eating and shopping, there are plenty of attractions well worth taking in. The leading sights are grouped here by district, with most located near the heart of the city and the Singapore River which flows through it. Many of the older neighborhoods and attractions have been renovated, but there are also some areas that have escaped renewal and offer a window into old Singapore.

☛ SINGAPORE RIVER

A good place to begin your exploration of Singapore is at **Raffles Landing** on the northeastern bank of the **Singapore River**. A white statue of Sir Thomas Stamford Raffles, located near the Empress Place Building, presides over the river shore, marking the site where the colonial founder first landed in Singapore in 1819. This statue, unveiled in 1972, is a later copy of the original dark bronze statue located nearby, in front of the Victoria Theatre and Concert Hall. The "black" Raffles monument dates from Queen Victoria's Golden Jubilee Year (1887). The **Victoria Theatre and Concert Hall** consists of two historic buildings joined by a clock tower; Singapore's old Town Hall (1862) is on the left and the Queen Victoria Memorial Hall (1905) is on the right. The complex is now the venue for concerts and art exhibits. Meanwhile, the **Empress Place Building**, next to the "white" Raffles statue, will reopen its doors in February 2003 as the main wing of the Asian Civilisations Museum. Built in 1864–65, Empress Place was once the headquarters for Raffles' employer, the East India Company.

In the block immediately north of Raffles Landing is a series of grand colonial buildings occupying the sites Raffles

The river bank where Singapore's visionary founder, Sir Stamford Raffles, first stepped ashore in 1819.

himself designated for government offices. The **Old Parliament House** dates from 1827, a two-story mansion that served as Singapore's courthouse until the completion of the Supreme Court up the street. In 1965, this old building (the oldest government building in Singapore) became the Republic's seat of Parliament. In 1999, Parliament moved to the modern gray complex next door. Singapore's other primary public offices lie just north of Parliament. The **Supreme Court**, opened in 1939 (but closed to the public) was Singapore's last classical edifice. It occupies the site of the legendary Hotel de L'Europe, once the city's most elegant place to stay, as Rudyard Kipling and other early travelers have attested. Next door is **City Hall**, built in ornate neo-classical style in 1929; this is where the Japanese surrendered to the British in 1945 and where Lee Kwan Yew later declared Singapore's independence from British rule.

Across the street to the east of these government buildings, just north of Raffles Landing, is a large field known as the **Padang** (Malay for "field") where Raffles planted the

25

Singapore Highlights

Singapore River Cruises ply the river down to Marina Bay daily from 9am to 9pm (recorded narrative; admission), with departures from the jetties at Parliament House next to the Victoria Theatre, at UOB Plaza next to the Raffles Place MRT, and near the Hotel New Otani at Clarke Quay. See page 24.

The Singapore History Museum (93 Stamford Road; Tel. 6332-3659; admission) is the city's best display of colonial and Straits Chinese artifacts. Open Tuesday–Thursday, Saturday–Sunday 9am–6pm, Friday 9am–9pm, closed Monday, with free guided tours in English at 11am and 2pm (additional tours at 3pm on Saturday and Sunday). See page 34.

The Singapore Art Museum (71 Bras Basah Road; Tel. 6332-3222; admission) is one of Southeast Asia's top contemporary art galleries. Open Tuesday–Thursday, Saturday–Sunday 9am–6pm, Friday 9am–9pm, closed Monday, with free guided tours in English at 11am and 2pm (additional tours at 3:30pm Saturday and Sunday). See page 35.

The Asian Civilisations Museum (39 Armenian Street; Tel. 6332-3015; admission) is strong on Chinese and Peranakan displays. Open Tuesday–Thursday, Saturday–Sunday 9am–6pm, Friday 9am–9pm, closed Monday, with free guided tours in English at 11am, 2pm, and 3:30pm (additional tour at 2:45pm Saturday and Sunday). See page 36.

The Raffles Hotel (328 North Bridge Road; free) is a stately establishment and the **Raffles Hotel Museum** in its shopping arcade is stuffed with memorabilia of Southeast Asia's most famous hotel. Open 10am–7pm daily. See page 40.

The Sri Mariamman Temple (244 South Bridge Road; free) is the city's oldest Hindu Temple (built in 1827), where the faithful still walk on burning coals at special festivals. Open daily 7:30–11:30am, 5:30–8:30pm. See page 42.

The Fuk Tak Chi Museum (Telok Ayer Street, Far East Square; free) is a former temple that now serves as the gateway to Chinatown. Open daily 10am–10pm. See page 44.

The Sultan Mosque (North Bridge Road; free) is Arab Street's main attraction and Singapore's largest Islamic shrine. Open daily 9am–1pm; Friday 9–11am, 2:30–4pm. See page 52.

The Malay Cultural Village (39 Geylang Serai; Tel. 6748-4700; admission) gives a taste of Peranakan and Malaysian customs, arts, history, and foods. Open daily 10am–10pm, it is only crowded at weekends, when live performances take the stage. See page 58.

The Singapore Botanic Gardens (Cluny Road; Tel. 6471-7361; free) have a superb display of the flora and fauna of southeast Asia. Open daily 5am–midnight. See page 58.

The National Orchid Gardens (Cluny Road, inside the Singapore Botanic Gardens; Tel. 6471-9955; admission) has the world's largest orchid display. Open daily 8:30am–7pm. See page 58.

Mandai Orchid Gardens (Mandai Lake Road; Tel. 6269-1036; admission) is Singapore's most popular orchid farm. Open daily 8:30am–5:30pm. See page 59.

Orchidville (10 Lorong Lada Hitam, Mandai Road; Tel. 6552-7003; free) is Singapore's newest large orchid farm, with worldwide shipping from its greenhouses. Open Monday-Saturday 9am–6pm, Sundays and holidays 9am–4:30pm. See page 59.

The Singapore Zoological Gardens (80 Mandai Lake Road; Tel. 6269-3411; admission) is one of the world's top zoos, employing an "open zoo" design using concealed moats and vegetation instead of fences and concrete structures. Open daily 8:30am–6pm, it is adjacent to the Night Safari, an even larger after dark zoo. Combination tickets are sold at the main zoo entrance for both attractions. See page 65.

Night Safari (80 Mandai Lake Road; Tel. 6269-3411; admission), the world's first night zoo, employs a tram and walking trails for a fascinating close-up look at nocturnal creatures that you never normally see. Open daily from 7:30pm to midnight, it is adjacent to the Singapore Zoo, where combination tickets are sold for admission to both zoos. See page 67.

British flag and ordered the ground cleared. It has long been the site of the members-only **Singapore Cricket Club**, founded in 1852, but is best remembered as the place where the Japanese military rounded up the entire European population of Singapore for interrogation in 1942.

Even with these architectural reminders of colonial Singapore, there's little about the Singapore River area that resembles the scene Raffles and the early British traders witnessed. Gone are the mangrove swamps, sultans' palaces, and the floating skulls deposited by pirates. Gone, too, are the godowns (warehouses), junks, and coolies that would line the shores. The muddy river has been cleaned up, and the picturesque shophouses across the river on **Boat Quay** have been renovated and brightly painted. The massive skyscrapers on the southeast bank, in **Raffles Place**, the heart of Singapore's financial district, now define modern Singapore's skyline.

The **financial district** has been located here since Raffles drew it up on his town plan in 1822. A handful of grand neo-Renaissance banks and office buildings remain, dwarfed by modern giants of finance such as UOB Plaza and Republic Plaza (two of Singapore's tallest buildings, both attaining the maximum-permitted height of 280 m (918 ft), or about 66 stories). Singapore's financial towers have been designed by international architects (such as I. M. Pei), but always in accordance with traditional Chinese principles of *feng shui*, which dictate the most propitious locations, shapes, and decorative flourishes of the city's Western-styled high-rises.

You can board a bumboat at the jetties near Raffles Landing, Raffles Place MRT, or Clarke Quay for a narrated tour of this riverside panorama of colonial and modern Singapore. The leisurely sail downstream and back passes beneath the historic **Cavanagh Bridge**, built of iron rails

Where to Go

from Scotland in 1868 to join the financial and administrative districts that Raffles had envisioned. Still open to pedestrians, the bridge now leads to the grand and lavish **Fullerton Hotel**, once the General Post Office, built in 1928. The Hotel stands on the site of old Fort Fullerton, which guarded the entrance to Singapore from 1829 to 1873.

An underpass below the Fullerton Hotel emerges at **One Fullerton**, a gleaming new restaurant and nightlife hub overlooking the waterfront. At the north end of One Fullerton is the new **Merlion Park**, where the Merlion statue — the city's mascot with the head of the proud lion and body of a mermaid (concocted as a tourism booster in 1964) — was moved recently. In the background is the hedgehog-like silhouette of the stunning **The Esplanade — Theatres on the Bay** performing arts center. Due to open in October 2002, the S$600 million center is a realization of Singapore's aspiration to be the performing arts hub of Asia.

The Cavenagh Bridge of 1868 links the Victorian-era colonial district to the high-rise financial district.

Singapore

The bumboats will give you a view of these newest changes in Singapore's ever-changing cityscape as they pass into **Marina Bay**. Marina Bay is actually an inner harbor created by a succession of massive land-reclamation projects that include Collyer Quay and Clifford Pier to the south and **Suntec City**, a new business, convention, and shopping hub, and the The Esplanade — Theatres on the Bay complex to the north of the river's mouth. The bumboats circle Marina Bay briefly, giving passengers a glimpse of the world's busiest port, where container ships and supertankers lie at anchor as far out as the horizon.

One area south of the Singapore River, adjacent to lower Marina Bay, that has lost much of its color to urban remodeling is **Raffles Place**, where a large MRT station was constructed. Raffles had designated this area as Commercial Square in his original master plan, and Commercial Square was at one time a vibrant place, surrounded by banks and godowns that led directly to the sea. Most of its old buildings have long since disappeared. The biggest loss has been

Outdoor dining in Boat Quay backed by high-rise towers.

Where to Go

Telok Ayer Market, an 1894 Victorian fantasy of an emporium fashioned out of cast-iron from Scotland. While the market was not destroyed, but fully reconstructed and reopened in 1990 as **Lau Pa Sat Market**, the new shops and fast-food outlets are lackluster at best. There's little of distinction left inside, though the market is still a wonder from the outside, and the nearby Cross Street night market is well worth a visit for its down-to-earth food stalls.

More successful restorations have been carried out on the quays (pronounced in Singapore as "keys") along the Singapore River. Raffles originally ordered the creation of five quays, or embankments, created by landfill. Collyer Quay and Raffles Quay were built south of the river's mouth; Boat Quay, Clarke Quay, and Robertson Quay lined the river inland through the heart of the city. The commercial river traffic that these quays were built to service has since died out (the last river trader sailed away in 1983). Today the quays have been gracefully restored, so that you can now follow the river promenades and walkways from quay to quay, sampling what each has to offer.

Boat Quay runs on the southwest side of the river between the Cavanagh Bridge and Elgin Bridge (which was constructed in 1925 to connect the Chinese and Indian communities). It was a landfill project, built with soil removed from what is now Raffles Place, a project that Raffles oversaw personally in 1822. Boat Quay alone soon handled most of Singapore's trade. The merchants vied to build their shophouses here. The taller the shophouse, the wealthier the owner. Renovation of the old shophouses and godowns was initiated in 1983, in a successful attempt to revitalize Singapore's riverside. Several of the renovations are highlighted by grand interiors filled with furniture and artifacts of the colonial era; all are brilliantly painted. Boat

Quay has become Singapore's favorite outdoor dining and drinking venue. The cafés, international restaurants, bars, and nightclubs are among Singapore's best.

Clarke Quay, upriver from Boat Quay, on the north bank, was the site of scores of 19th-century godowns built by colonialists and Chinese alike. Several Chinese merchants became millionaires through their trading businesses at Clarke Quay. One old godown, River House, has been preserved in Block A of the Clarke Quay renovation, as has an old pineapple cannery in Block C. Block E is a new mall built on the site of the Whampoa Icehouse (the ice being imported from Boston in the early days). Unlike the Boat Quay renovation, however, the Clarke Quay redevelopment has left little trace of the Singapore River's colorful past.

Robertson Quay, located a little farther upriver than most tourists usually venture, but a pleasant shoreline walk from Clarke and Boat Quays, contains three godowns (once owned by regional banks) that are still quite picturesque. There's a fine view of them from the trendy high-tech hotel dining room on the fourth floor of the Gallery Hotel. In fact, the Robertson Quay area is especially trendy and pleasantly uncrowded. Located on the north side of the river off Clemenceau Bridge, the cafés and shops are often upscale. Nearby Mohamed Sultan Road has become Singapore's hottest nightclub and disco site, making Robertson Quay a popular haunt after dark. The river, once the very life blood of Singapore, has become a pleasant promenade, where labor and trade are forgotten.

THE CIVIC DISTRICT

For decades, visitors to downtown Singapore have referred to the area north of the lower Singapore River as the Colonial District, and for good reason. This is where many

Where to Go

Preservation and Destruction

When Singapore achieved independence in 1965, the economy was in shambles. Like every developing nation, Singapore put modernization and economic progress on the front burner; anything that stood in the way, from historic neighborhoods to colonial architecture, was simply razed. By the 1970s, Singapore was on its way to achieving spectacular prosperity, but it had obliterated much of its irreplaceable past, and visitors were beginning to complain that Singapore lacked character and color.

By the 1980s, Singapore began to heed its critics. Historic temples, office buildings, Peranakan mansions, shophouses, and godowns were more often spared demolition and restored with grace.

By the late 1980s, the government focused on four areas for conservation (Boat Quay, Little India, Kampong Glam, and Chinatown). More areas have been added. For some, these efforts at preservation come too late; for others, the preservation schemes themselves have been directed too often by commercial, rather than aesthetic, considerations.

Today's visitors must decide for themselves whether Singapore's recent conservation measures have transformed the once-gritty and vibrant colony into what approaches a Disneyesque museum, or rescued some outstanding architectural and ethnic treasures from neglect.

of the colonial-era buildings and the museums of Singapore history stand. Raffles had staked out the north side of the river for the British colonialists from the beginning, ordering the building of offices, banks, hotels, churches, and clubs there. He even built his house in what is today the Civic District, on the top of Fort Canning hill. The leading colonial architects of the time were George Coleman, who consulted with Raffles on many designs, and John Bidwell, who brought neo-Renaissance plans to the Raffles Hotel, the Goodwood Park Hotel, the Victoria Theatre, and many other preserved buildings. The house Coleman built for himself early on suffered the fate common to many older buildings in modern Singapore; it was demolished to make way for the Peninsula Hotel.

Fortunately, much has been spared in what has been renamed the **Civic District**, making it the most important colonial neighborhood for travelers to stroll. The collections inside the Singapore History Museum, the Asian Civilisations Museum, and the Singapore Art Museum are superb. The historic Armenian Church, The Cathedral of the Good Shepherd, and the lovely CHIJMES complex are beautiful. The Maghain Aboth Synagogue, Fort Canning, and the Raffles Hotel are major monuments to Singapore's colonial years. All lie between the Dhoby Ghaut and City Hall MRT stations on and just off Stamford Road, in the heart of civic Singapore.

The **Singapore History Museum** is dedicated to explaining the island's past. The collection is housed in one of Singapore's most impressive colonial edifices, opened in 1887 (Queen Victoria's Golden Jubilee) as the Raffles Library and Museum. Renamed the National Museum in 1969, then the Singapore History Museum in 1999, it presents a walking tour through Singapore history using dioramas on the first floor. There's also a Straits Chinese Gallery with Malay-Chinese artifacts and a Peranakan house, the Revere Bell (donated to Singapore's St. Andrew's Cathedral in 1843 by Paul Revere's daughter), and an extensive jade collection once owned by the founder of the Tiger Balm company. A high-definition 3-D film presentation, combining animation and historical film footage, gives the Singapore perspective on its own lively history. The museum also organizes walking tours of historic and ethnic Singapore, conducted monthly by local experts, that are worth pursuing.

Modern sculpture at the Singapore Art Museum.

The **Singapore Art Museum** is also housed in a superb colonial structure, the former St. Joseph's Institution. The dome in the central hall dates from 1867, the curved wings from 1906, and other additions from as late as 1914, much of it designed by the French Catholic priests who presided over St. Joseph's. This Christian Brothers school was taken over and refurbished by the Singapore National Museum in 1987. The art collection, which includes sculpture and installations as well as paintings, is contemporary, representing the works of Southeast Asia's leading modern artists. It ranks among the finest contemporary art museums in the region, and it is worth touring just to see the splendid chapel and other restored interiors.

Singapore

☞ The **Asian Civilisations Museum**, the newest of Singapore's three national museums, opened in 1997 in the renovated Tao Nan School building. Tao Nan, built in 1910, was the first Singapore school to employ Chinese as the language of instruction. The collection focuses on the two cultures that dominate Singapore, the Chinese and the Peranakan, with the city's most extensive display of cultural artifacts from these two groups. The Peranakan exhibit includes displays of batik and betel-chewing implements; the Chinese exhibit has a reconstructed scholar's study. Special exhibits of Asian culture open throughout the year. The main wing of this museum is due to open in the Empress Place building in 2003.

In addition to the three national museums, the Civic District has outstanding examples of the religious institutions favored by colonials. The Convent of the Holy Infant Jesus, known most widely by its acronym, **CHIJMES** (pronounced "chimes"), may be the most beautiful architectural legacy of Christianity in old Singapore. The buildings on this walled block of Queen Street (between Bras Basah Road and Middle Road) were constructed in different eras, but the restored Gothic Chapel, dating from 1890, is the most spectacular piece. Designed by Father Nain, a French priest, it is thoroughly medieval in design and ornamentation — and ornate it is, as striking a work in the Gothic style as exists in Asia. This chapel now serves aptly enough as a concert hall.

Other notable buildings in the complex (a private development) include the Caldwell House (1841), a mansion designed by George Coleman; the St. Nicholas Girls' School (1913); and new creations that blend in well while hosting boutiques, galleries, trendy restaurants (Grappa's, Lei Gardens) and nightspots. The "Gate of Hope" entrance was

Where to Go

once where the destitute and desperate left newborn babies in the hope that the convent would adopt them.

Among fine churches still standing in the Civic District are the **Cathedral of the Good Shepherd** (1846), a Renaissance-style building between Queen and Victoria Streets with six porticoed entrances and a high wooden ceiling; the gothic brick **Wesley Methodist Church** (1909) on Fort Canning Hill; the **Church of St. Peter and Paul** (1870) on Waterloo Street, with its original bells; and the spacious **St. Andrew's Cathedral** (1856) on St. Andrew's Road (directly above the City Hall MRT station), with its white tower, spires, and commemorative wall plaques.

The most popular Christian shrine with visitors, however, is the **Armenian Church** (1835) on Coleman Street. It is not merely Singapore's oldest church; it is colonial architect George Coleman's masterwork. The circular interior chambers are grand and well-proportioned. The Armenian Church once served thousands of refugees fleeing the war between Russia and Turkey; it was constructed using the labor of Indian convicts. The churchyard contains the graves of two of Singapore's most famous Armenian residents: the Sarkies, who built Raffles Hotel, and Agnes Joachim, whose orchid (Vanda Miss Joaquim) is the national flower.

The colonial Cathedral of the Good Shepherd.

Worship at the Maghain Aboth Synagogue.

Not all colonials were Christian. A number of far-flung immigrants were Jewish. The **Maghain Aboth Synagogue** at 24-26 Waterloo Street, built in 1878, was Singapore's first synagogue, and it remains the city's most active. The current Jewish congregation numbers a few hundred, but at one time Waterloo Street and Middle Road teemed with Jewish households. By 1830, nine Jewish families (peddlers and dealers in spices among them) had settled in Singapore, but the Jewish population didn't swell until the 1930s, when over 2,500 Jews, mostly immigrants, were counted. At the time, it was said that the Jews owned half the rental properties in Singapore. The names of many Jewish families who helped develop the city are inscribed on the map today (Wilkie Road and Solomon Street, for example).

The Maghain Aboth Synagogue remains quite active, with evening services at 6:45pm and morning services at 9:30am Monday–Friday, 9:15am on the Sabbath (Saturday), and at 8am on Sundays and holidays. The interior is quite warm, striking, and traditional, with mezzanine seating for women, an altar girded with oil lamps, and an unusually large number of torah scrolls. Attached to the synagogue is an elaborate *mikvah* (a purifying bath for women), posted with rules for its use. A kosher food market takes place daily (closed on Saturday, and on Jewish and public holidays).

Where to Go

Tours of the synagogue, topped off by a sampling of Jewish foods, are sometimes offered through the Singapore History Museum. For more information on the Jewish community in Singapore, contact the Jewish Welfare Board (Tel. 6337-2189) or check the website <www.singaporejews.com>.

Forming the western boundary of the Civic District and overlooking the Singapore River is **Fort Canning Park**. In Raffles' day, it was known as Forbidden Hill (Bukit Larangan), the site of a royal palace built by a Sumatran prince in 1297. Java's forces destroyed the sultans and their palaces on the hill in 1392. The ghosts of these sultans were believed to haunt the hill, the curse not broken until William Farquhar cleared the summit and erected a cannon there for defense in the early 19th century. Raffles built a bungalow on Fort Canning in 1823, occupying it for almost a year. Until Singapore surrendered in World War II, the hill was a British military command post.

Today Fort Canning has venues for drama and performing arts, the holy tomb of Sultan Iskander Shah (last ruler of pre-colonial Singapore), and nature and history trails for those seeking a green refuge from the busy downtown. The main attraction is the **Battle Box** (Tel. 6333-0510; open 10am–6pm except Monday; admission), the bomb-proof bunker of 26 rooms and corridors 9 m (30 ft) underground, where British Lt-General Percival decided to surrender to the Japanese armies (15 February 1942). The bunker has been equipped with wax robots and film projections to recreate the events leading to Singapore's fall. Other attractions include a 19th-century history trail, the ASEAN Sculpture Garden, the original fort gate (1867), and a replica of the 19-hectare (47-acre) spice garden Raffles established in 1822 as the "experimental and botanical garden" of colonial Singapore.

Singapore

Raffles' name is popularly preserved today in the **Raffles Hotel**, perhaps the most famous hotel in Asia. Despite the name, it was not founded by Raffles at all, but by the Sarkie brothers, Armenian immigrants who put together a small new hotel in 1887. The writer Joseph Conrad was among the first to check in, followed in 1889 by Rudyard Kipling, who praised the food but not the accommodations. The Sarkies went on an upgrade rampage (characteristic of Singapore through the centuries, it seems), adding the Tiffin Room, Palm Court, and the Billiard Room by 1902. It was in the Billiard Room that the last tiger (an escapee from a nearby circus) was shot in Singapore.

Monarchs, film stars, and Nobel prize-winning authors have all stayed at Raffles, including Charlie Chaplin and John Lennon. This did not protect the hotel from the neglect and decay that led, in 1989-1991, to the government declaring it a National Monument and providing for a massive facelift. The result is controversial: the hotel has been reconstructed in a highly upscale manner and surrounded with an arcade of designer-label shops. But perhaps this all-suite hotel is to the 21st century what Raffles was to the early 20th century and its grand visitors.

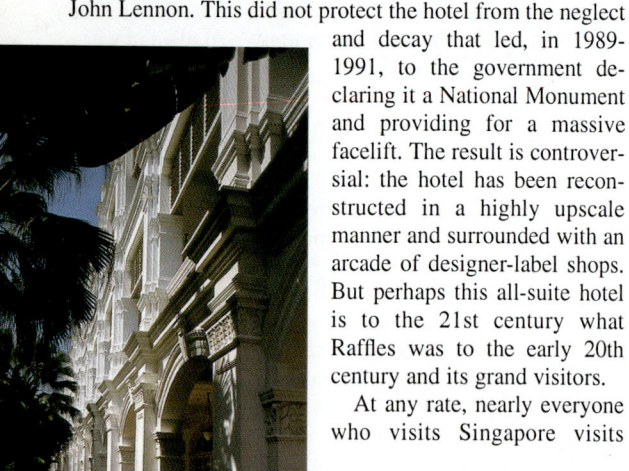

At any rate, nearly everyone who visits Singapore visits

Symbol of Singaporean elegance: the Raffles Hotel.

Raffles. The Bar & Billiards Room is probably the most romantic spot for a drink. The open courtyards at the rear are good for tropical dining. The Raffles Hotel Museum on the third floor, next to the gift shop, is small, but has an intriguing collection of colonial-era hotel artifacts. The Raffle Hotel's **Long Bar** — where the Singapore Sling was invented in the early 1900s — may be nothing like the atmospheric original (despite its ceiling fans and peanut-shells on the floor), but then, how could it be in an age of mass tourism?

CHINATOWN

Sir Thomas Stamford Raffles drew the general outlines of Singapore's Chinatown back in 1822, just after the first boat-loads of Chinese immigrants from Fujian Province landed at the mouth of the river. The Chinese found hard labor jobs along the river; their fresh water source was a well on Spring Street; gangs, triads, and opium dens became a way of life. **Chinatown**, then as now, occupied a large area immediately southwest of the Singapore River. The Hokkien traders settled along today's Telok Ayer and Chulia Streets; the Teochew fishermen congregated near Boat Quay; and the Cantonese merchants built shophouses along Pagoda and Temple Streets. The tangle of provincial neighborhoods was always confusing; Chinatown is still a labyrinth today. Visitors are almost as likely to come across a Hindu temple or Islamic mosque as a Buddhist shrine in this sprawling district (which was saved from the complete ravages of the wrecking ball only by the rise of the preservation movement in the 1980s).

A good place to begin your wanderings through the heart of the Chinatown maze is not at a Chinese site at all, but at the **Sri Mariamman Temple** on South Bridge Road,

Love Potions

Aphrodisiacs are something of a Singapore obsession. Just check out the pharmacy at the Imperial Herbal Restaurant near Raffles for a selection of the best in Chinese love potions, from deer-penis wine to seahorse tonic, which some locals drink daily. Even geckos, prolific during mating season, end up in a potent green liquor. Along Arab Street, Malaysian medicinal houses favor onions for prolonging sexual stamina. Indian pharmacists, relying on the Tantric traditions and the Kama Sutra, will boil asparagus and treacle in milk and ghee, spiced with liquorice. You'll find a storehouse of the ingredients used in Indian aphrodisiacs at the Mohd Mustafa Store on Syed Alwi Road in Little India, and in Chinatown any pharmacy worth its ginseng will stock a fertile line of sexual herbs, tonics, and antlers to lift up a flagging libido.

between Temple and Pagoda Streets. South Bridge Road was the traditional site of Cantonese merchants who specialized in herbal medicines and gold jewelry, shops still to be found here. Sri Mariamman is Singapore's oldest and most important Hindu temple, dating from 1827. Mariamman is a Hindu god celebrated for curing serious diseases, such as cholera. The pagoda-like tower, decorated in representations of the Hindu gods, is called a *gopuram*. The interior is noted for its ceiling paintings, and the temple is the site for the Thimithi ceremony in which believers walk on burning coals.

A stroll down Temple Street (off South Bridge Street) takes one past plenty of Chinese souvenir shops (lacquerware, silks, Tiger Balm ointments) to Trengganu Street, now an outdoor street vendors' mall, but previously an opera street with theater stages and houses of prostitution. Trengganu Street terminates at Sago Street, another colorful

Where to Go

shopping area with its Chinese pharmacies, rattan weavers, kite-makers, and carpenters. Just off Sago Street is Banda Street, the best place to shop these days for paper offerings meant to be burned at funerals. The offerings, which come in the shapes of Rolls Royces, laptop computers, cell phones, and credit cards, as well as cash, are sent heavenward in smoke to the deceased, who apparently have not renounced consumerism in the afterlife.

Temple Street and the parallel Pagoda Street both lead westward in short order to New Bridge Road and Eu Tong Sen Street, currently the almost impenetrable construction zone for a much needed new Chinatown MRT station. Worth a detour at 48 Pagoda Street is the new **Chinatown Heritage Centre** (open daily 10am–7pm; admission), which showcases the lifestyles and rich traditions of the Chinatown of yesteryear.

Eu Tong Sen Street is the location of several of Chinatown's most interesting and gritty shopping arcades (People's Park Complex and People's Park Centre, with its textile dealers), as well as the Yue Hwa Department Store (formerly the Great

The Sri Mariamman Temple: ritual bathing.

Club Street shophouse turned into a nightclub.

Southern Hotel) with its Chinese clothes, and souvenirs. Most of Chinatown's attractions, however, lie east of South Bridge Road, which was constructed in the 1830s by prisoners imported from India.

Ann Siang Road and **Club Street**, once the haunt of letter-writers for hire, are filled with finely restored shophouses (as well as a few colorful unrestored specimens). The style is not entirely Chinese. The carved decorations and swinging "cowboy doors" are Malaysian in origin, while the Georgian windows and art deco touches are European. The tiled roofs are strictly Chinese, of course. Club Street also contains an array of restored terrace homes and shophouses, most built after 1900, many with ornate balconies. True to its name, Club Street housed an array of trade associations, but is now a nightspot, with plenty of bars and restaurants.

Club Street rises and plunges into Upper Cross Street, the location of Far East Square and China Square Food Centre, two large food and shopping malls that replaced the traditional food and shopping streets many Singapore Chinese grew up with. On the east side of this modern complex is Telok Ayer Street, worth strolling for its cluster of national monuments, beginning with the **Fuk Tak Chi Museum** (open daily 10am–6pm; free). This is the first Chinese temple ever built in Singapore (1825). The museum consists

Where to Go

of original and restored pieces of the old temple complex, reopened in 1998 as a kind of side entrance to the malls. Tua Pek Kong, the Cantonese and Hakka God of Wealth, is the main deity worshipped here. The temple combines aspects of Buddhism and Daoism.

One block south down Telok Ayer Street are three shrines in a row. First comes the **Nagore Durgha Shrine**, built between 1828 and 1830 by Muslims from southern India. Next is the **Thian Hock Keng Temple** (Temple of Heavenly Bliss), built between 1839 and 1842, which traces its origins to the first Chinese immigrants, who built this elaborate Daoist shrine to their maritime protector, Ma Chu Poh, the Goddess of the Sea. It employs granite pillars from south China, blue tiles from Holland, and cast-iron railings from Scotland. Although the main altar is Daoist, a rear chamber dedicated to Guanyin, Goddess of Mercy, is Buddhist. Before landfills intervened, this temple stood on the edge of

Chinese pharmacies sell everything from tea to powders purporting to have aphrodisiacal qualities.

the sea. The last temple on Telok Ayer Street is **Al-Abrar Mosque**, known as the Indian (or Chulia) Mosque, which opened in 1855. Singapore's remarkable mingling of ethnic and religious groups is quite visible in the consecutive placement of these three diverse places of worship, although only the Thian Hock Keng Temple receives visitors regularly.

There are still many sights in Chinatown just off the main tourist routes. The **Eu Yan Sang Medical Hall** (267 South Bridge Road; open 9am–6pm except Sunday), which opened in 1910, is the ultimate Chinese pharmacy. Here visitors can sample or purchase everything from ginseng tea to wines purported to have aphrodisiacal qualities.

The **Tanjong Pagar Conservation District**, at the south end of South Bridge Road, is another area of similarly restored shophouses and upscale shopping and dining, and the site of the Jinrickshaw Station building (1903), where rickshaws began congregating in the 1880s. By the 1920s, coolies were pulling over 10,000 rickshaws daily, a major means of getting around Chinatown until after World War II, when motorized trishaws took over. Tanjong Pagar's reconstruction began with the Jinrickshaw Station and 32 nearby

Prayers at Thian Hock Keng Temple (the Temple of Heavenly Bliss), built by the first Chinese immigrants.

shophouses. Over 200 shophouses have been meticulously restored along Neil Road, Murray Terrace, Craig Road, Duxton Hill Road, and other historic lanes.

☛ LITTLE INDIA

Among the first Indian settlers were 120 assistants and soldiers who sailed into Singapore in 1819 with Raffles. They lived in Chinatown along Chulia Street, the original Indian quarter, but as cattle-raising increased along the Rochor River to the north, India's immigrants congregated in an area bisected by Serangoon Road which is now

Shop for a stylish sari in Little India.

known as **Little India**. Hindus are in the majority here among Indians, although Tamil Muslims are well-represented; both groups, however, are dominated numerically by Chinese, who make up almost three-quarters of Little India's population. This is perhaps the most colorful downtown neighborhood to stroll in Singapore, its back streets and thoroughfares marked with the "five-foot ways," or covered corridors, that arch out from the shophouses.

For a walking tour of Little India, start at the **Little India Arcade** on Serangoon Road, opposite the Tekka Centre (a market and vendors' emporium). The arcade, converted from shophouses in 1982, has a "cultural corner" with period photographs of Serangoon Road and illustrations of the food, fashions, and customs (including bangles, forehead dots, and henna designs) of Singapore's Indian community, most of whom first immigrated from the Calcutta and

Hindu devotee at the Sri Veeramakaliamman temple.

Madras in South India. The Little India Arcade has shops selling *saris* (colorful wraps) and *cholis* (short-waisted blouses), as well as sweets, medicines, betel nuts, carvings, and brassware. There's also a "hawker center" inside, where you can dine cheaply on a variety of Indian dishes.

From the Little India Arcade you can wander north up Serangoon Road, exploring the flavorful side streets as they come. Campbell Lane is filled with five-foot ways and shops selling woodcarvings, furniture, and musical instruments. Dunlop Street has textile and dress shops, as well as small, exotic groceries. A few blocks down Dunlop Street (near the Perak Street intersection) is the **Abdul Gaffoor Mosque**, a Singapore national monument. Most Singaporean Indians are Hindu, but the Muslim faithful congregate here on Fridays. The mosque (except for the prayer hall) can be visited if you dress respectfully (with your legs covered). Dating from 1859, the present brick structure, blending Arabic and European styles, opened in 1910. A block north, on Perak Street, is the **Church of True Light**, an Anglican place of worship built in 1951 to serve Chinese Christian residents of Little India.

Returning to Serangoon Road, famous for its goldsmiths, you can take a brief detour down Cuff Road for a look at the

Spice Grinder Shop (open daily 9am–6:30pm except Mondays), a noisy, but fragrant enterprise, one of the last remaining in Singapore, where the freshest mixes of spices, flours, and betel nuts are custom-ground. A little farther up Serangoon Road, at Belilios Road, is the **Sri Veeramakaliamman Temple**, constructed by Bengalis in 1881. This is one of Singapore's finest Hindu shrines. Dedicated to Kali, the Hindu Goddess of Power, it is packed with fervent followers on the holy days — Tuesdays and Fridays. Visitors are free to enter this temple (open daily 9–11:30am, 5–9:30pm), which is noted for its coconut-cracking custom. Devotees often break a coconut before entering to denote the breaking of their ego. Cracked shells are tossed into the aluminum receptacles under the *gopuram* (sculptured gate tower). This temple interior is fascinating for the number of Hindu symbols it employs. Fresh coconut and mango leaves above the entrance are for purity and welcome; the lotus represents human striving for spiritual perfection; banana offerings indicate abundance.

A good way north up Serangoon Road, at Perumal Road, is another national monument: the **Sri Srinivasa Perumal Temple**, built in 1855, has a vast prayer hall to honor Vishnu, the supreme Hindu god (open daily 6:30–noon and 6–9pm). Nearby, at 366 Race

Cracked coconuts symbolise the surrender of selfish ways.

Course Road, which runs parallel to the west of Serangoon Road, is the **Sakyamuni Buddha Gaya Temple**, better known as the **Temple of 1,000 Lights** (open daily 8am–4:45pm). This Buddhist shrine, maintained by Thai monks, is one of the most popular religious shrines in Singapore. Its centerpiece is the seated Buddha statue, 50 feet tall and weighing in at 300 tons. The Buddha is surrounded by light bulbs that light up every time a donation is made. The scene is spectacular, if kitsch, complete with several Hindu statues and two bright yellow tigers posted as guards outside.

The temple across the road, at 371 Race Course Road, is **Leong San Temple** (Dragon Mountain Temple), a less fanciful place of Chinese worship. It's a Daoist shrine, but dedicated to the Goddess of Mercy, Guanyin (who is actually a Buddhist deity). Ancestral tablets are stored at the back, and there's a prominent statue of Confucius here — who was neither Daoist nor Buddhist, Hindu nor Muslim. Next door, in a ramshackle house oozing character, a local spirit medium resides.

Farther still up Serangoon Road, at Boon Keng Road, is the **Central Sikh Temple**, a formidable modern concrete structure with a dining hall on the first floor and a domed prayer hall on the second floor, where Sikhs go to pray and relax under the cool fans during the heat of the day. Colorful wall posters recount the history and principles of the Sikh religion (open daily 10–11am, 1–2pm, and 4–5pm).

KAMPONG GLAM

Named after the glam trees that once grew here, the **Kampong Glam** district (north of the Civic District and the Singapore River) was the historic seat of the Sultans. Settled by Muslims from Malaysia and the Bugis from Indonesia,

When the Spirit Moves You

Mediums, who channel messages from the afterlife while in a trance, are surprisingly common in Singapore. They operate in small temples and in their own medium houses, which resemble rundown Daoist temples. Many, if not most, Singaporeans seem to believe in their power. Mediums are frequently called upon to forecast upcoming lottery numbers. Their trances are flamboyant. Mediums often gyrate rapturously, swoon, fall, and dash from point to point. Piercings are nearly mandatory. Long needles are inserted through elbows, wrists, hands, mouths, or tongues, to be withdrawn as the trance abates, usually leaving no blood or visible wound. Two temples, both west of Chinatown off Zion Road, where you're most likely to see a medium at work are the small **Giok Hong Tian Temple** (Temple of the Heavenly God) at Zion and Havelock roads, a Daoist shrine where throngs of worshippers take a joss stick home with them on New Year's Day for good fortune, and the **Monkey God Temple (Tse Tion Tai Seng Yeh)**, at the corner of Eng Hoon Street and Tiong Poh Road, a family shrine that has grown as the temple medium's flock has grown. On the Monkey God's birthday in the fall, a number of mediums congregate at the Monkey God Temple, pierce themselves, and enter into sustained, dramatic trances.

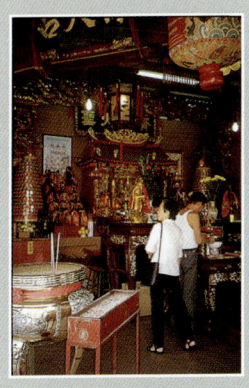

this neighborhood has maintained a pronounced Islamic character, especially around Arab Street.

☛ **Arab Street** is the traditional home of Singapore's textile dealers, and there are still many small silk and batik stores here, as well as sarong shops. Leather goods, caneware, fishing gear, and shiny metalwork are also for sale in the shophouses protected from the direct sun by the five-foot ways. Haji Lane, running parallel southwest of Arab Street, is fascinating, too. Kazura Perfume Shop (51 Haji Lane) has a fine display of decanters; the perfumes are non-alcoholic versions of Western standards.

☛ The leading attraction is the **Sultan Mosque**, located between Arab Street and North Bridge Road at the end of Bussorah Street. Bussorah Street was converted into a pedestrian mall in 1997, with a few restaurants and rather characterless retail shops on the ground floor. It makes for a serene entrance to the Sultan Mosque, an impressive edifice with its massive onion-shaped golden dome and corner minarets. A National Monument, rebuilt and reopened in 1928, this is Singapore's largest mosque; visitors are welcome to observe (but not enter) its grand prayer hall.

The adjacent **Istana Kampong Glam**, at Kandahar Street, is under reconstruction as a Malay Heritage Centre. Built about 1840, it served as the residence of Malay royalty. There are two old Malay cemeteries north of here. On Victoria Street is the location of the Malabar **Jamah-Ath Mosque**, famous for its blue tile work. Northeast of the Sultan Mosque, at 4001 Beach Road, is the **Hajjah Fatimah Mosque**, now a National Monument, built in 1846 by the Malaysian wife of a Bugis merchant as a private residence. Its remarkable architecture mixes European and Chinese influences with a Malaysian minaret that resembles the white spire of a

Where to Go

cathedral. The minaret is off the plumb, leading some to dub it "the leaning tower of Singapore."

Bugis Street, south of the Arab Street area on Victoria Street, was Singapore's most notorious after-dark hangout until it was razed in 1985 to construct the Bugis MRT station. Attempts to recreate the good old bad days have so far failed, despite belated government attempts to replicate the seedy shophouses and bars — even going so far as to invite back the original transvestites (as roving guides) that had made Bugis Street Singapore's little Sodom and Gomorrah. Now, in place of a street internationally renowned for prostitution and drag queens, there is Parco Bugis Junction, a glitzy new shopping mall with a glassed-over and temperature-controlled shopping street, and, across Victoria Street from the subway station, a clothing and junk market that is somehow seedy without being interesting.

What is worth seeing in the Bugis neighborhood are the two shrines two blocks to the west on Waterloo Street. The **Kuan Im Tong Hood Temple** is one of the most crowded in

Little India street stalls sell garlands of scented flowers in colours that symbolise purity, happiness, and prosperity.

the city. The Buddhist Goddess of Mercy, Guanyin, presides here. Rebuilt in 1982, the temple architecture is not the attraction – rather it is the flower-sellers outside and the supplicants inside. This is a fine opportunity to watch worshippers offer incense and flowers to the goddess, kneel and shake fortune sticks in a box, then consult with the priests as to the meaning of the stick that first appears. From lottery numbers to the prospects for offspring, the goddess tries to unravel the future from 6am to 6:15pm daily. Just next door, at 152 Waterloo Place, is a Hindu shrine, the **Sri Krishnan Temple**, highly ornamented, with incense sticks out front for the convenience of worshippers who spill over from next door.

Temple to consumerism: Orchard Road shopping mall.

ORCHARD ROAD

Orchard Road, running west from the Civic District and Dhoby Ghaut MRT station, is Singapore's best known shopping avenue and dining district, though it has some sights worth seeing, too. The name of this glitzy road goes back to the 1840s, when Captain William Scott established his nutmeg and pepper plantation on the slopes. Tigers roamed the hills along Orchard Road until 1846; fifty years later, the land was tamed and some of Singapore's richest families had built their estates and terrace homes here.

The most notable cluster of these historic residences is on **Emerald Hill**, the site of one of Singapore's first and most impressive preservation projects. A stroll up Emerald Hill Road from Peranakan Place is a walk into Singapore's stately colonial past. The terrace houses were constructed

Where Late the Sweet Birds Sang

Singapore is always changing, meaning that popular — even venerable — sights can disappear in a blink. One long-standing tourist haunt, the informal and very much local birdcage "park" at Tiong Bahru and Seng Poh Roads (west of Chinatown), has vanished. The neighborhood gentlemen once gathered here every morning, hanging their ornate birdcages on hooks outside a small café, where they listened as their beloved (and highly pampered) thrushes and merboks belted out a few songs. Sundays, especially, drew crowds to this singing bird corner, where the café did a landrush business with coffee, tea, and snacks. Where have the birds and their Chinese owners flown? To the suburbs, to new government housing blocks, to make way for urban renewal (the area still has blocks of low-rise public housing from the 1950s). A few bird fanciers do remain in the area, and a bird supply store is holding on tenaciously, despite the exodus of regular customers. Sharing the square with this old store is the colorful **Wee Tin Temple** (Wei Zhen Miao), where the God of the Underworld is worshipped and the Tiger God is called upon to devour "small-minded" enemies.

between 1902 and 1930 on the site of a nutmeg farm by a variety of architects using a plethora of Malaysian, Peranakan, Chinese, and European styles. The original owners were wealthy Straits Chinese merchants. Pastel hues, fancy plaster work, ornate grills, shuttered windows, bat-shaped openings, tiled overhangs, and carved wood characterize many of these graceful exteriors. There are a few galleries and restaurants among the houses, which allows a glimpse of their colonial-period interiors, but most of the restored terrace homes and shophouses are expensive private residences. The carved door-fences (*pintu pagar*) are designed for ventilation and privacy.

Orchard Road is also the address of the **Istana**, the palace that is home to Singapore's president. Indian convicts did the heavy work on this government estate in the late 1860s, which is unfortunately closed to visitors except on New Year's Day, Chinese New Year's Day, Hari Raya, Labor Day, and Deepavali. If you are there on the first Sunday of any month, you can catch the changing of the guard at the Istana gates (starting at 5:45pm). More accessible is the **Goodwood Park Hotel** at 22 Scotts Road, a national landmark built in 1900 as the Teutonia Club for German colonialists. The Goodwood vies with the Raffles as Singapore's most luxurious historic hotel. Resembling a Rhineland castle with its eight-sided Bavarian tower, it was occupied by Japanese officers during the war, serving as the War Crimes Court later. Celebrities who have spent the night here include Anna Pavlova and John Wayne.

On the south side of Orchard Road (west of Fort Canning) are three religious sites. The **Chesed-El Synagogue**, less active than Maghain Aboth Synagogue on Waterloo Street (see page 38), opened in 1905 on Oxley Rise. It served as the private synagogue for Menasseh Meyer, a real-estate tycoon.

Chettiar Temple on Tank Road, also called Sri Thandayuthapani, was rebuilt in 1884. It was traditionally the temple favored by *chettiars*, Indian money-lenders from Madras, and its *gopuram* (tower) is one of the most lavishly carved pantheons of Hindu gods in Singapore. The interior is equally ornate. The annual Thaipusam Festival procession from the Sri Srinivasa Perumal Temple (see page 94) ends here, with coconuts, symbolizing the ego, smashed open on the courtyard pavement. The **Singapore Buddhist Lodge** (Hong San See) on Kim Yam Road, an active and spacious complex, serves free vegetarian lunch to its worshippers.

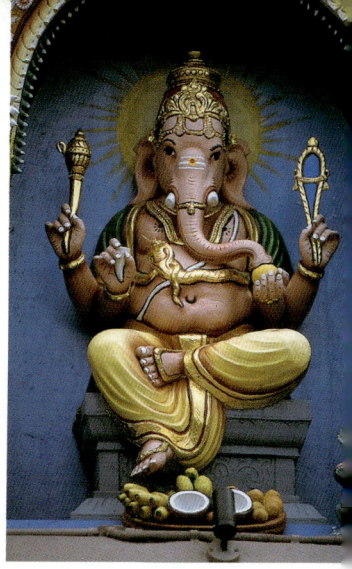

Ganesh, the popular elephant-headed Hindu god of prosperity.

GEYLANG SERAI

When the British transformed Singapore into a trading colony, many Malays took up residence in **Geylang Serai**, east of the city center. The district still has a strong Malay character, complete with old bungalows, terrace houses, and Peranakan shophouses, especially along Joo Chiat and Koon Seng roads near the Paya Lebar MRT station. Singapore's largest red-light district and a cluster of "love hotels" are located in the *lorongs* (alleys) here. So, too, is the **Geylang Serai Market** near Geylang

Road, selling fish, fruit and clothing. Across from the market is the **Malay Cultural Village**, a theme park recreation of kampong stilt-house architecture, with cafés and cultural shows. There is a museum in the village featuring a fine display of Malay wedding customs. This is a good place to see demonstrations of kite-making, batik work, and kampong games.

ZOOS, PARKS, AND ORCHIDS

Some of Singapore's top attractions lie outside the urbanized centers and neighborhoods of downtown Singapore, including the island's world-renowned zoos, bird parks, nature reserves, and the orchid farms which form a much appreciated counterweight to the city-state's metropolitan-laden landscape.

The **Singapore Botanic Gardens** on Cluny Road, just west of Orchard Road, are the nearest major green preserve to the downtown district. The 128-acre (52-hectare) site of exotic gardens and jungle forests is free to visitors, except for the **National Orchid Garden**, the world's largest display of Singapore's signature bloom.

Singapore's Botanic Gardens are packed with colour.

Where to Go

The Botanic Gardens were opened in 1859 as a repository of Southeast Asian flora and fauna. The gardens begin at Swan Lake, surrounded by palms and rubber trees, then lead past an 1860 bandstand and a topiary garden. A new extension features an arboretum of trees organized by their continent of origin, from Australia to Africa. The National Orchid Garden, opened in 1996, has over 2,000 varieties, including an ample display of Singapore's national flower, the purple Vanda Miss Joaquim. A visit here includes a glimpse of the VIP orchids, named after the dozens of dignitaries who have visited Singapore. The Botanic Garden's gift shop is a favorite of visitors, many attracted by the gilded blooms made into jewelry.

Singapore's most often-visited flower farm is the **Mandai Orchid Gardens** on Mandai Lake Road, well north of the downtown area, near the zoo. Operated by a private grower, the Mandai Orchid Gardens exports cut flowers and plants to over 30 countries worldwide. The water garden includes tropical plants from many countries that do well in Singapore's climate, including heliconia and traveler's palm. Gardeners are usually hard at work tending the orchids, which require intensive cultivation.

A new alternative for orchid-fanciers is **Orchidville**, also located on Mandai Road, opened in 1993 by the Phua family, who had been successful pig farmers in the past. Their greenhouse approach to creating a humid environment for growing orchids seems to have paid off, extending the lives of their blooms. Visitors are welcome to view some of the two million pots of orchids; visitors can also cut their own flowers to take home or arrange overseas shipping of purchases. Each pot has a life expectancy of five years; 400,000 new plants are bred each year to maintain the stock, which makes Orchidville the largest such enterprise in Singapore.

A mossy denizen of the garden undergrowth.

Gardens of a different order are maintained at the **Chinese and Japanese Gardens** (1 Chinese Garden Road; Tel. 6261 3632; open daily 9am-6pm; admission). The Chinese garden reflects several classical styles and employs twin pagodas, arched bridges, an extensive bonsai display, elaborate rock works, a teahouse, and even a marble boat like the one in Beijing's Summer Palace gardens. From the Chinese Garden visitors cross a bridge into the Japanese Garden with its carefully raked Zen rock gardens, stone lanterns, pavilions, and pools. These adjacent gardens, charging a single admission, are seldom visited these days. They have a quiet, almost desolate look, but they are crowded during Chinese New Year and the Lantern Festival.

Far more lively, but also fallen on hard times lately, is the most Chinese of the world's theme parks, **Haw Par Villa**, also known as **Tiger Balm Gardens** (262 Pasir Panjang Road; Tel. 6872-2003; open daily 9am-7pm; free). There's hardly a native resident in Singapore who wasn't taken here as a child. This park was opened in 1935 by Aw Boon Haw, who built a mansion for his younger brother, Aw Boon Par, on the summit. The Aws made a vast fortune based, in large part, on sales of Tiger Balm.

The amusement park lining the slopes below the villa is lined with garish, and often grotesque, statuary telling

Where to Go

stories from classical Chinese mythology, literature, and folklore. These illustrated fairy tales frequently have a moral, which might explain why parents have taken their children here for several generations, exposing them to the traditional values, mostly Confucian, of imperial China. The statues originally numbered over a thousand, and there were scores of tableaux showing fantastic heroes and villains representing aspects of good and evil, engaged in the primal struggles of life and death.

The Japanese destroyed the mansion during their occupation and it was never replaced, but the park itself was rebuilt. The government then acquired it in 1985 and leased it to a private firm that tried to update the old theme park with high-tech displays and rides. This renovation was a failure. Recently, Haw Par Villa has begun to reverse the tide and return to its roots. The rides are gone, and hundreds of statues are coming back, including King Kong-sized gorillas and a Statue of Liberty. No admission is currently charged, and local families seem to be finding their way back to this nostalgia-laden attraction. The best sites in the park are the huge tableaux of classic Chinese stories that stand at the summit, and the cave called the Ten Courts of Hell, where appropriate punishments for each type of earthly sin are gruesomely and surrealistically inflicted on life-size figures by their tormentors.

Classical Chinese architecture at the Chinese Garden.

Singapore

> ### The Feather in Singapore's Cap
>
> Despite its reputation as a concrete island of high-rises, Singapore has over 350 species of birds to delight even the most casual bird-watcher. Early morning, around 7am, is prime spotting time. The Bukit Batok Nature Park is the current hot spot, famed for the endangered Straw-headed Bulbul, first discovered here in 1996. The laced woodpecker and white-crested laughing thrush provide plenty of auditory entertainment here, too. The Sungei Buloh Nature Park has observation blinds by a mangrove where there's a breeding colony of herons in residence from August to March. The quiet isle of Pulau Ubin, with its mangroves and rain forests, is home to parakeets, owls, kingfishers, and hornbills. A good place to start a bird-watching expedition is at the Visitor Centre in the Bukit Timah Nature Preserve, where illustrated field guides are for sale. And from September to March, the white cattle egret takes its winter holiday in Singapore, arriving from as far north as Japan and as far west (or east) as France.

Jurong BirdPark

The largest bird park in Southeast Asia, **Jurong BirdPark** (2 Jurong Hill; Tel. 6265-0022; open daily 8am-6pm; admission) is located on 20 hectares (50 acres) of parkland far west of downtown, and is a favorite amusement park of local and visiting families. More than 8,000 birds, representing 600 species, reside here. The hornbill collection is one of the largest in the world. Also the largest in the world is a 30-m (98-ft) high artificial waterfall located at the end of a walk-in aviary where 1,500 birds fly freely. The park can be explored on foot, but there is a monorail (admission) that links the myriad displays. Among the more notable displays are the Southeast Asian Birds Aviary, where a tropical thunderstorm is simulated at noon; the Nocturnal House, where snowy owls, night herons, and kiwis can be observed in the darkness; and a Parrot Paradise, where the park's most colorful and friendly residents congregate. Other attractions include an air-conditioned hummingbird gallery, a penguin pool with 200 of the flightless birds representing five species, and a lake with hundreds of pink flamingos. A highlight is the dramatic open-air auditorium "all star bird show" at 10am, 11am, 3pm, and 4pm daily.

It is best to arrive early, before the heat of the day. Visitors can then watch the 9:30am breakfast show at the Songbird Terrace ("Pelicans, Parrots & Prata") and enjoy a breakfast buffet (8–10:30am), dining to the sounds of songbirds. A resident parrot serves as the breakfast fortune-teller, picking cards from a deck.

Recently the park, open since 1971, has been emphasizing the ecological dimensions of the endangered habitats these

Making friends with some of the delightfully colorful and companionable species at the Jurong Bird Park.

exotic birds inhabit in the wild. One new display, the Riverine Exhibit, offers a river's edge view of over 20 duck species fishing and nesting in a pristine niche. Their underwater activities, including diving for fish, can be observed through a wide glass portal on a path that runs below the river's surface.

Bukit Timah Nature Preserve

If you want to see what outdoor Singapore looked like when Raffles and the first Westerners arrived (and for some 100 million years before that), head for the **Bukit Timah Nature Reserve** (177 Hindhede Drive; Tel. 6468-5736; open daily 7am–7pm; free), located in the northern portion of the island. This spacious park (164 hectares; 400 acres) harbors Singapore's largest surviving old-growth rain forest, native vegetation that once covered most of the island. Bukit Timah is a marvelous place to hike, with a series of well-marked trails winding through the hillsides. Bukit Timah is the name

Like most of the animals in Singapore Zoo, the African lions enjoy spacious and naturalistic enclosures.

of the park's summit, the highest point in Singapore at 163 m (535 ft).

Bukit Timah boasts more tree species than are found in the whole of North America. The ecosystem has never been cleared or affected by an ice age. The towering tropical trees (such as the *seraya* and *pulai*) provide a canopy for palms, rattans, and over 80 species of ferns. Flying lemurs, long-tailed macaques, pangolins (spiny anteaters), mouse deer, giant forest ants (one-inch long), banded woodpeckers and tit babblers are sometimes heard but not often seen. You may see only a few squirrels during a brief hike, as the forests are extremely dense, and most of the life of the forest is in the tree canopy overhead, rather than on the ground.

Bukit Timah is just 12 km (7 miles) from the city, bordering the Bukit Timah Expressway and several government housing complexes. It has barely escaped cultivation and clearing. Established as a forest reserve in 1883, it was the only such forest that escaped logging. Pressure for land development mounted, but in 1951 Bukit Timah and several other areas were set aside for the preservation and propagation of native flora and fauna. The Visitor Centre has hiking maps and offers a self-guided exhibit of the park's ecosystem, now managed by the National Parks Board. An uphill hike from the Visitor Centre at the park entrance to the Summit Hut, with its picnic shelter and active lookout on stilts, takes less than 30 minutes each way. The four main trails (and side trails) lead to valleys and large quarries where swimming is permitted. There's also a fine 6-km (3.7-mile) biking trail encircling the parklands.

Singapore Zoo

One of the world's best zoos, the **Singapore Zoological Gardens** on Mandai Lake Road (open daily 8:30am–6pm;

Getting to know the gentle elephants at the Zoo.

admission), north of downtown, houses over 3,000 animals and reptiles on its 28 hectares (69 acres). One thing that sets the Singapore Zoo above most is its "open zoo" compounds in which even the most ferocious of the animals seem to roam in their native environments with little in the way of fences and screens placed between visitor and wild resident. Concealed moats, cascading streams, and vegetation help serve as barriers, although a few glass-fronted enclosures are employed for species that can leap over walls. There are still some old-fashioned compounds of concrete, too, but it is hoped these will be rebuilt and opened up in coming years. A lucky few, including some langurs, lemurs, and tamarins, are allowed to range freely throughout the zoo.

Not to be missed are the animal shows, staged at 10:30am. 11:30am, 12:30pm, 2:30pm, and 3:30pm daily in selected areas (with additional shows on weekends at 1:30pm, 4pm, and 5pm). Most shows are held in the Shaw Foundation Amphitheatre, where sea lions, reptiles, or primates take their turns on stage throughout the day. The elephant shows take place as scheduled at the Elephant Ride Area. Animal

Where to Go

Friends Shows get under way at the Children's World enclosure at 12:30pm daily, with an additional show at 4pm on weekends. A "Zoo Inside and Insights" tour is held at 2:30pm on Sunday only, a rare chance to view the kitchens and the animal hospital during a behind-the-scenes stroll. Note, too, that many animals, from lions and jaguars to monkeys and Komodo dragons, are fed on a regular schedule (times posted daily beyond the zoo entrance), as this can lead to some exciting shows, too. Even the tigers are likely to take a plunge in their pool when the feeding crew arrives. The zoo's most popular shows are Breakfast with an Orangutan (9am daily) and Tea with an Orangutan (4pm daily, except Sundays).

To avoid the crowds, make your zoo visit in the morning (the zoo opens at 8:30am) on a weekday. If you are combining a visit with the Night Safari next door (highly recommended), it is best to take your zoo tour in the afternoon, 3 or 4 hours before the 6pm closing, and then walk over to the Night Safari for a cafeteria dinner before the self-guided and tram tours commence at 7:30pm. Both the zoo and the Night Safari are crowded all day every day, as these are two of Singapore's top international attractions.

Night Safari

The world's first night zoo, Singapore's **Night Safari** (open daily 7:30pm–midnight; admission), adjacent to the zoo, has been the island nation's top attraction since opening in 1994. Covering 40 hectares (99 acres), it is a completely different experience. Beginning at dusk (7:30pm), a series of trams, most with English-speaking narrators aboard, encircles the eight geographical zones on a 3.2-km (2-mile) paved roadway. Passengers can disembark and take a closer and more leisurely look at the animals in their open enclosures by following one of three walking trails. In addition, there are two 30-minute stage shows, called "Creatures of the Night," featuring a civet, an otter, a cougar, and a python (which is let loose under the seats of the audience!). The preserve stays open until midnight, and many of the visitors find the later hours less crowded and more interesting.

Set in a dense tropical forest, next to an inlet of the Seletar Reservoir, the Night Safari is a subtly-lit preserve inhabited by over 1,200 animals representing about 110 species from Asia, Africa, and South America. Over 90 percent of the animals in the wild are nocturnal, so this is a chance to see how the animals behave after the heat of the day and the sunlight have vanished.

Perhaps the most entertaining creatures are the fishing cats, slightly larger than domestic felines, who take the plunge to capture trout in a small stream just inches from the pedestrian bridge that passes through their wooded area. The focused, incandescent lighting used to illuminate the fishing cats and other animals makes everything visible to humans, but does not distract the creatures of the night, who are often quite active and seemingly unaware of passers-by. Visitors are separated by natural barriers (moats, vegetation, near-invisible wires) and the lighting system resembles moonlight. Cameras are allowed but flash is prohibited.

The twilight world of the Night Safari has given those not inclined to bars, nightclubs, and stage shows an after-dark alternative that no other city can beat.

ISLAND EXCURSIONS

Singapore is an island of islands. Some of its 58 nearby islets are now used for petroleum refining and storage, but a few make for excellent day trips, reached by cable car or bridge,

Where to Go

in the case of Sentosa, or by ferry or bumboat, in the case of Kusu and Pulau Ubin.

Sentosa

Singapore's fantasy island, **Sentosa**, just south of the main island, is connected by the 710-m (½-mile) Causeway Bridge (toll). An alternative is to go by the **cable car** (admission) that drifts 91m (300 feet) above the harbor (passing the container wharves and dry docks) into the heart of the island's vast theme park (admission). The cable cars (Tel. 6270-8855) depart continuously from the World Trade Center daily starting at 8:30am; the last cable cars return from Sentosa at 9pm. Autos and taxis can use the bridge from 7am until midnight daily. The cable car also makes a longer trip from Mount Faber to Sentosa and back daily from 8:30am to 9pm and offers sky dining (in a glass-bottomed

Views of the world's busiest harbour from the cable car that links downtown Singapore to the island of Sentosa.

cable car) every Friday and Saturday night 6:30–8:30pm (Tel. 6277-9640 for reservations). Another option is the **ferry** (Monday–Friday 9:30am–9pm, Sat–Sun 8:30am–10pm) which connects the World Trade Center and the Sentosa Ferry Terminal (near the musical fountain) every 20 minutes.

Sentosa originally served as headquarters for the British military, based at Fort Siloso. The island, originally known as Pulau Blakang Mati, was renamed Sentosa in the 1980s and developed as a resort, attracting over one million visitors annually to its beaches, golf courses, wax museums, aquarium, amusement centers, and resort hotel (the Shangri-La Rasa Sentosa).

Sentosa Island's Dragon Court.

Western visitors may find the theme island too much like a hygienic Disneyland to be interesting, but its recreational opportunities are among Singapore's best, and there are some historical and cultural attractions that are worth touring in their own right.

A free monorail encircles the island and gives an overview of Sentosa, from the swimming lagoons on the south side to Fort Siloso and Underwater World on the north. Many of the main attractions are within walking distance of the cable car station at the heart of the northwest portion of the island. Here, elevators whisk visitors to the mouth and

Where to Go

crown of the 37-m (121-ft) high statue of the **Sentosa Merlion** (admission), from where there is a fine view of the island and busy harbor. At night, the Merlion becomes the focus of a towering light show, complete with smoke and laser lights worthy of a psychedelic dragon. Nearby is a dazzling computer-controlled **Musical Fountain** that performs into the night. Other minor attractions are the **Butterfly Park**, with 2,500 butterflies and an exhibit of unusual insects, and **Orchid Fantasy**, a modest display accentuated by a pond teeming with magnificent koi carp.

Visitors with children may want to make the rounds of Sentosa's amusement centers (all charging separate admissions) located east of the cable car terminal (at monorail station 1). The attractions here include **Cinemania**, where visitors are strapped into computer synchronised seats that simulate every bump and hair-raising moment of roller coaster rides and speed races; and **Volcanoland**, which takes visitors on an amusement park ride into the heart of a manmade Mayan volcano that erupts every 30 minutes.

Sentosa's best attraction near the cable car terminal (monorail station 4) is **Images of Singapore** (open daily 9am–9pm, admission), a fine museum housed in the colonial-style former military hospital. This tells Singapore's history and displays its various cultures using life-sized dioramas, artifacts, films, and replicas of old street scenes. Among the highlights are a recreated opium den, an extensive festival showcase, and the **Surrender Chambers**, which bring to life Singapore's formal surrender to the Japanese in 1942.

Sentosa's other historical display is **Fort Siloso** (monorail station 3; admission), built in the 1880s by the British to defend Singapore. The audio-olfactory-visual displays along the underground passages, the 6-inch guns, and the video

Close encounters with the creatures of the deep blue sea at Sentosa Island's Underwater World theme park.

games tell the history of the fort from its construction through to its fall in World War II.

Sentosa is also the location of **Underwater World** (monorail station 2; open daily 9am–9pm; admission), a small but excellent aquarium with a submerged acrylic tunnel at its heart. Visitors ride through the main tank on a "travellator," or moving sidewalk, while observing the comings and goings of 5,000 sea creatures overhead and on all sides — including turtles, stingrays, sharks, sea cows, and monstrous eels, which seem to engulf the "undersea" viewers. Underwater World also oversees the **Dolphin Lagoon**, where visitors can enjoy a show or wade in and come face to face with Indo-Pacific Humpback Dolphins, also known as pink dolphins for their unique coloration.

Sentosa levies a small basic admission for all visits. Most of the attractions, which are generally open 9am–7pm daily, levy additional admissions. Various package tickets can be purchased at some hotels and at the World Trade Centre. Sentosa Island (Tel. 1800-736-8672) is open daily from 6am to midnight. Taxis must pay a surcharge to use the Causeway Bridge. The monorail and Sentosa buses are free, and bicycles are for rent on the island. There is no MRT subway station serving Sentosa.

Pulau Ubin and Kusu

A popular escape for Singapore residents is provided by nearby **Kusu Island** (Pulau Tembakul) and **St. John's Island** (Pulau Sakijiang Bendera). On weekdays, both islands are uncrowded, and both offer picnic grounds, changing rooms, and swimming beaches. St. John's, the larger of the two, has little else but picnicking and swimming, although the concrete promenades on the shoreline are fine for a stroll and watching the heavy ship traffic in the harbor. Kusu has more to see, including a turtle sanctuary, the Tua Pekong Temple at the ferry wharf (a favorite of Daoist worshippers) and the Keramat Kusu Islamic temple at one end of the island, popular with childless couples who come here to pray for offspring.

The island ferry, departing from the World Trade Centre, makes a circuit, going first to Kusu, then to St. John's, twice daily Monday through Saturday (10am and 1:30pm) and six times on Sunday (starting at 8:45am). The last ferries depart St. John's at 2:45pm (6:05pm on Sunday) and Kusu at 3:15pm (5:50pm Sunday). The schedule changes from year to year (Tel. 6271-9520 for the latest information). Visitors use the ferry to make a survey of both islands.

If time allows a visit to only one of Singapore's little islands, the best choice is **Pulau Ubin**, where some of the last vestiges of old Singapore hang on by their fingertips.

Singapore

Part of the fun is getting there on a bumboat, hired for a nominal fee at Changi Point (reached from downtown Singapore via taxi or MRT to Tanah Merah station, then bus number 2). The bumboat takes about 20 minutes to make the crossing. The village at the wharf on Pulau Ubin hasn't changed in decades, with its cluster of *kelongs* (Malay fishing huts), but there are now several businesses renting bicycles by the hour, the ideal way to get around the little island. There's an information kiosk (Tel. 6542-4108) at the village entrance that provides useful maps. Local taxi drivers offer guided tours, too, but you'll have to negotiate the fare.

The mangrove forests and coconut palm groves are impressive, as are the duck and prawn farms and granite quarries (Pulau Ubin means "Stone Island"). The Ma Chor Temple, just above the seashore outside the village, is worth a hike up for its view.

A slow tour of the islet will reveal the remains of rubber

In the sleepy fishing village of Pulau Ubin you will find the last vestige of old Singapore and its traditional ways.

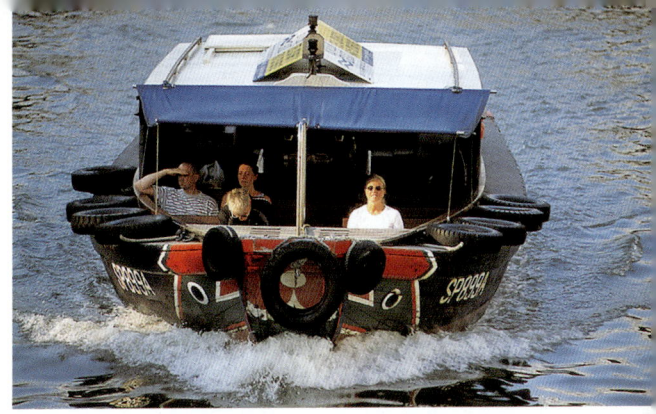

Island transport is provided by fast and nimble bumboats.

plantations, some small Islamic mosques, a half dozen tiny fishing villages where the houses are on stilts, jungle farms, and fruit trees laden with papaya, mango, jackfruit, and durians. Long-tailed macaques and wild boars also live here, but they are difficult to spot. The island population has dwindled to 200, as the granite quarry business has declined. Some residents still farm and fish, some serve the tourist trade, and a few run seafood restaurants. Noordin Beach on the north side of the island attracts swimmers and overnight campers, while the quarries that have filled in with water attract adventurous swimmers.

The remote, undeveloped western end of the island is the preserve of an Outward Bound School. The village and jetty are leisurely places to hang out, enjoy a cool drink, and perhaps talk with the locals in the most relaxed setting Singapore offers. Bumboats leave the isle for Changi Point on no fixed schedule; they simply sail as soon as they have 12 passengers. For those who wish to spend a night, accommodation is available at Ubin Lagoon Resort (Tel. 6542-9590).

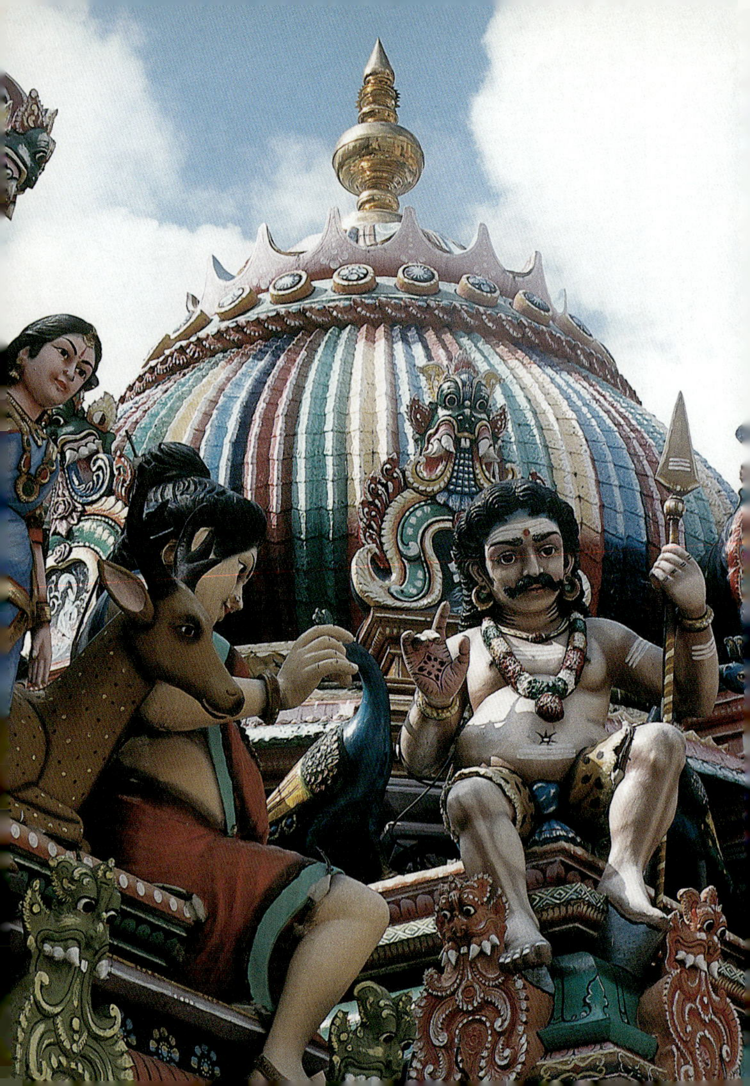

WHAT TO DO

Shopping and eating are the lifeblood of Singapore. Visitors will find an endless array of places to do both, economically or in high style. Singapore now has an increasing number of venues for entertainment and sports, too, as well as an extensive calendar of annual festivals that are well worth attending. Nor does any other city offer a better opportunity to introduce children to the pleasure and cultures of Asia.

SHOPPING

If Singapore has a national pastime, it is shopping. The downtown is stuffed with air-conditioned malls, department stores, and boutiques, and the ethnic neighborhoods offer additional street markets and small shops. Most shopping centers and shops are open from 10am to 9pm daily (sometimes later at weekends). Credit cards are widely accepted. Most larger stores and shops do not engage in bartering, but vendors with stalls in markets often do. Many retailers can provide overseas shipping. Insist on written confirmation of the purchase and buy shipping insurance unless covered by your credit card. Shop around to compare prices and quality; test an item before purchasing.

As a free port, Singapore offers a great deal of tax-free shopping. A Goods and Services Tax (GST) of 3 percent is levied, and the GST can be refunded to you if you spend a total of SGD300 (so long as each purchase is SGD100 or more) at participating shops. Look for the "TAX FREE FOR TOURISTS" logo in shops and have the clerk fill out a tax-free shopping check with your purchase.

Present all copies of the shopping checks, the goods, and your passport to the Customs office at the airport.

Singapore

Then cash your Customs-approved checks at the nearby Cash Refund counter (or mail your stamped checks in later for a refund check, or a credit to your credit card). Brochures covering the details of GST refunds are available in the arrival halls of the Changi Airport, at 2,500 affiliated shops, and in many hotels (Tel. 6225-6238).

> **English is the common language in this country of many languages**

The Civic District is dominated by shopping centers, department stores, and malls. Some of these are big; others are bigger; and among the biggest is **Suntec City Mall** (3 Temasek Boulevard), the current favorite among Singaporeans. Suntec's shopping towers are much like those in Western cities, although the goods can have an Asian flavor. Its shopping is divided into four zones, with lifestyle products in one and food courts and expensive

Money-Back Guarantees

Merchants at Changi Airport, providing your last chance to shop in Singapore, now offer two guarantees. The first is on price. If you find you paid more at the airport than at one of the dozen downtown department stores and major shops on their list, they'll give you a double the price difference refund. The second guarantee is simpler. If you bought the wrong gift or changed your mind, they will give you a full refund, no questions asked, if you return the item and receipt within 30 days. You can do this even after leaving Singapore; shipping costs will be refunded as well. For details, fax or write the manager of the airport shop. For details, write Commercial Division, Civil Aviation Authority of Singapore, Singapore Changi Airport, P.O. Box 1, Singapore 918141.

From huge international malls to traditional shophouses in Little India and Chinatown, Singapore has it all.

boutiques in others. The central, circular Fountain of Wealth puts on shows throughout the day. Billed as the world's largest fountain, its waters flow downward instead of shooting upward, since the traditional Chinese belief is that water represents wealth and the shopkeepers here want the water flowing directly into their shopping center. Since most of the offices in Suntec's towers are doing high-tech and internet work, Suntec is referred to locally as Singapore's vertical silicon valley. Other large malls and shopping arcades in this area include **Millenia Walk** (9 Raffles Boulevard), with its Duty-Free Shop, and the **Marina Square Shopping Mall**, with its bargain boutiques.

Approved Shops
Shops displaying the CaseTrust (CT) logo are accredited as reliable and honest by the Consumers Association of Singapore.

The **Raffles Hotel Shopping Arcade** contains art galleries and Raffles Hotel souvenirs at its museum shop. The **Raffles City Shopping Centre** nearby is linked to Suntec City Mall by an air-conditioned walkway, appropriately dubbed the CityLink Mall.

Orchard Road is another major downtown shopping strip, renowned for its upscale international stores. Among the leading shopping centers are Wisma Aria (435 Orchard Road), Ngee Ann City (391 Orchard Road), Paragon (290 Orchard Road), and Centrepoint (176 Orchard Road), home of Robinson's, Singapore's oldest department store (since 1858). The Far East Plaza (14 Scotts Road) has clothing at low prices. Tang's Department Store (320 Orchard Road) is a delightful emporium with Chinese touches.

At the western end of Orchard Road, down Tanglin Road, the Tanglin Shopping Centre gathers together the city's largest selection of Persian rugs, antique maps, and Asian antiques. At the eastern end of Orchard Road, where it turns into Stamford Road, the Stamford Court and Stamford House specialize in modern furniture, while the shops in the Singapore History Museum, the Asian Civilizations Museum, and at the National Museums Shop (on Armenian Street) specialize in gifts and cultural souvenirs.

Traditional souvenir vendor on Clarke Quay.

What to Do

Other major commercial areas include Clarke Quay, with its 80 shops and an excellent flea market on Sundays (9am-5pm); the Jewellery Mart at Pidemco Centre; electronics at Sim Lim Square (1 Rochor Canal); and Bugis Junction, a street mall that retains its shophouse architecture, with a vendors' night market, Pasar Malam, nearby.

Singapore's ethnic neighborhoods offer more unusual shopping possibilities. **Chinatown** is headlined by Yue Hwa Chinese Products (70 Eu Tong Sen Street), a department store where the clothing, household goods, and crafts are all from China. People's Park Centre is filled with Chinese vendors willing to bargain, and People's Park Complex is a rundown arcade where textiles and clothing can be had for some of the best prices in town, if you're willing to bargain.

Little India is the area to poke around for bangles, gold jewelry, and silk saris. The Little India Arcade on Serangoon Road has over 50 small shops, and the nearby Tekka Centre (known locally as KK, or Kandang Kerbau) has a wet market on the first floor and scores of shops above selling saris, batiks, clothing, and brassware. At the intersection of Arab Street and Beach Road, take a look at Jamal Kazura Aromatics, where hundreds of bottled fragrances (all without alcohol) are on display.

The streets of Little India and the Arab District are a delight to stroll, and the small shops offer unusual goods, usually at decent prices (ask for discounts). The Geylang and Katong districts also offer bargains. This is a Malay area, and the Muslim merchants at the Malay Market (Joo Chiat and Changi Roads) handle a variety of goods, from batiks and silk scarves to cooking pots and prayer rugs.

Suburban shopping offers many of the same consumer goods available downtown, but often at much better prices.

Singapore

Here, amongst Singapore's towering housing estates, the malls serve the locals who live, eat, and shop within an easy walk. Known as the heartlands, these resident malls are becoming Singapore's new towns. Several of the heartlands are served directly by the MRT. The Century Square mall is at the Tampines station; Junction 8 is at the Bishan station; and IMM is at the Jurong East station.

The sad fact is that the prices in Singapore on many goods are equal to or higher than in Western countries. Better prices on the same goods are now found throughout Malaysia, Thailand, and Indonesia. Nevertheless, if you are not going to these countries to shop, Singapore may be your best chance to pick up Asian items. It never hurts to ask for a discount, either.

Bargain stores do exist in Singapore. The island's version of "dollar stores," where nothing on the shelves is over the one set price, make for interesting browsing. You'll find items you've never seen before. Keep an eye out for the Under S$2 Shops and the One.99 Shops in the malls, and Tang's Budget Corner in Tang's Department Store. Other discount chains include Sasa (for cosmetics), Export

Complaint Departments

Always efficient, Singapore has several means to rectify retailer malfeasance. You can complain to the Retail Promotion Centre, Block 528, Ang Mo Kio Avenue 10, #02-2387 (Tel. 6450-2114; fax 6458-6393) or you can contact the free online dispute resolution service offered by the E@DR Centre at <www.e-adr.org.sg>. A third choice is to contact the Small Claims Tribunal (Apollo Centre #05-00, 2 Havelock Road; Tel. 6535-6922; fax 6435-5994), where visitor complaints are heard on short notice and judgments are rendered on the spot.

Fashion, and Why Pay More. The Cavallino Recycle Shop (01-05 Tanglin Shopping Centre, 19 Tanglin Road) has designer fashions and accessories at half price. The Vintage Place (02-08 Pacific Plaza, 9 Scotts Road; 01-20 Plaza Singapura, 68 Orchard Road) sells new and used designer-name fashions and shoes at bargain-basement prices.

Special Shops

Shoppers for Buddhist art and **antiques** should check out Lopburi (01–03, Tanglin

Bugis Village market offers bargain-price shopping.

Place, 91 Tanglin Road; 11am–7pm, Sundays until 4pm). Certificates of authenticity and shipping are provided. There is a big cluster of antiques shops up the road at Tanglin Shopping Centre (19 Tanglin Road), including Antiques of the Orient (02-40), Akemi Gallery (02-07), Hassan's Carpets (03–01), Naga Art & Antiques (01–34), and Renee Hoy Fine Arts (01–44). Nearby, Antiquity Hands of the Hills carries Himalayan and Tibetan pieces (141 Tudor Court, Tanglin Road). Dempsey Road is also filled with many tiny, very fine antiques, carpet, and Asian collectible shops. Kwok Gallery (03–01 Far East Shopping Centre, 545 Orchard Road) has dealt in genuine Chinese dynastic pieces since 1918; and the Singapore Handicraft Centre (72 Enos Avenue) has stocked a complete range of Chinese carvings, paintings, medicines, and rosewood furniture since the 1940s

(Monday–Saturday 11am–6:30pm, Sunday 2–6pm). Pagoda and Mosque streets in Chinatown are also well known for their antiques stores.

Singapore's leading **bookstores** are Borders (Wheelock Place, 501 Orchard Road); Kinokuniya (Ngee Ann City, 391 Orchard Road), with its 20,000 comic books in Chinese, Japanese, and English; and the venerable (since 1908) MPH (71–77 Samford Road). An interesting alternative is the small, independent Select Books (03–15 Tanglin Shopping Centre, 19 Tanglin Road), the ideal place to find the Singapore and Southeast Asian books, travel guides, and academic studies that the big stores don't carry.

Among custom **tailors**, Coloc Tailor (02–29 Raffles Hotel Arcade, 328 North Bridge Road) can complete a suit in 24 hours. Gentlemen's Quarters (03–13 OUB Centre, 1 Raffles Place), in business for three decades, provides overseas shipping. Mohan's (02–60 Far East Plaza, 14 Scotts Road) tailors men's and women's fashions, with shirts starting from SGD30 and suits from SGD250.

For something different, find the Chinese **opera** supply shop, Eng Tiang Huat (284 River Valley Road; Tel. 6734-3738; open Monday–Saturday, 10am–6pm). Established in 1937, this shop is full of musical instruments, martial arts equipment, opera props and embroidered vests.

One of the best times to shop Singapore's retail shops and malls is during the Great Singapore Sale, which runs from the last week in May through June to the first week in July. There are good discounts on a wide range of goods during these six weeks.

ENTERTAINMENT

In addition to shopping, eating, and visiting the cultural attractions of Singapore (including Sentosa and the Night

Safari after dark), there is a growing nightlife scene, although it remains a tamer one than those found in some other Asian and Western capitals.

Singapore's **performing arts** programs bring international East and West entertainers to town. Current attractions are listed in the tourist magazines, such as *Where Singapore*, and in the daily newspaper *The Straits Times*. Check the Internet at <www.happening.com.sg> for updates. Tickets can be purchased through SISTIC outlets (Tel. 6348-5555; <www.sistic.com.sg>) and at Ticket Charge outlets (Tel. 6296-2929; <www.ticketcharge.net>).

Popular Chinese art form: traditional opera.

The Singapore Symphony plays at the Victoria Concert Hall. Visiting Western operas and ballet companies favor the Kallang Theatre. The Fort Canning Centre hosts dance troupes. Chinese opera and dance companies often perform in the larger Kreta Ayer People's Theatre and the World Trade Centre's auditorium. Singapore has a dozen of its own Chinese opera companies, which often perform on outdoor stages in Chinatown and at annual festivals, particularly at the Festival of the Hungry Ghosts in the early fall.

The completion of The Esplanade — Theatres on the Bay — gives Singapore a new world-class performing arts center, an entertainment landmark that many hope will rival Sydney's opera house.

Singapore

Late-night entertainment is spread across hundreds of nightclubs, discos, pubs, lounges, wine bars, and karaoke parlors. The dress code at clubs and discos is on the formal side (no jeans or T-shirts). The top nightclubs and discos are Zouk, a trendsetter with wine bar, disco, and video bar (17–21 Jiak Kim Street; Tel. 6738-2988; open Wed, Fri, Sat); Bar None (Marriott Hotel, 320 Orchard Road; Tel. 6831-4656; open daily), where live band Energy packs in the crowds; Brix (Grand Hyatt, Scotts Road; Tel. 6738-1234; open daily), a very happening place with beautiful people and special theme nights; the Hard Rock Cafe (02–01 HPL House, 50 Cuscaden Road; Tel. 6235-5232; open daily); and the world's largest Planet Hollywood (541 Orchard Road; Tel. 6733-5339; open daily). All have cover charges that usually include one or two drinks; most are open from about 7pm to as late as 3am. Other top dancing spots are the China Jump Bar & Grill (in CHIJMES, 30 Victoria Street; Tel. 6338-9388) and New Asia Bar (Swissotel The Stamford, 2 Stamford Road; Tel. 6431-5669; open Fri and Sat).

Singapore's climate is perfect for spending long lazy evenings in the outdoor cafés of Clarke Quay.

What to Do

The Mohamed Sultan Road strip near Robinson Quay, with its restored shophouses, has become Singapore's newest and hottest nightlife center, led by such upscale clubs and bars as Sugar, Club Eden, and the very stylish Orange, none of which close until 3am.

For those seeking a leisurely drink in the evening, perhaps some music, but not the energetic dance and disco venues of the clubs and discos, Singapore has a large number of stylish **bars and lounges**, many with outdoor seating. The exquisitely-restored Boat Quay shophouses on the Singapore River now house such establishments as Harry's Bar (28 Boat Quay), a favorite of Nick Leeson, whose financial misdeeds led to the fall of Barings Investment Bank; the very homey Mag's Wine Bar-Bistro (86 Circular Road); Fez (57B Boat Quay), a laidback candle-lit watering hole above Kinara North Indian restaurant; Molly Malone's Irish Pub & Grill (42 Circular Road); and the very Victorian "public house," Penny Black (26–27 Boat Quay). Just opposite the river is Bar Opiume (Empress Place Waterfront), which attracts a very stylish crowd. And further upriver is Clarke Quay, with its restaurants, bars and microbreweries.

CHIJMES in the Civic District at 30 Victoria Street offers an Irish Pub (Father Flanagan's), which also serves food apart from Guiness and Kilkenny, and Ocho's, a Spanish-themed tapas bar with a nice al fresco area and good sangria by the jug. Other popular Civic District haunts are Paulaner Brauhaus (01–01/02 Millenia Walk) and the very stylish Balaclava (01–01B Suntec City); a risque cabaret with stand-up comedy, Boom Boom Room (Far East Square, 130 Amoy Street); a trendy Absolut vodka bar, Fluid (11 Purvis Street); The Long Bar (Raffles Hotel) where Singapore Slings are must-haves; and the elegant Post Bar in the Fullerton Hotel (1 Fullerton Square).

Singapore

Orchard Road probably has more bars and lounges per block than any other street in Singapore, but the quieter places are on classy Emerald Hill, where you'll find a Spanish wine bar (Que Pasa), an international cocktail bar (No. 5), and just plain beer straight from the tanks of a 1910 Peranakan shophouse (Ice-Cold Beer). Tanjong Pagar, the restored shophouse area around Duxton Road near the financial district, has live jazz at JJ Mahoney, a wine bar at the Joy Luck Club, champagne and wine at the Bisous Wine Bar, and classic Chinese décor at Shui Hu. Sentosa Island offers surfside bars, including Sunset Bay, and the Mahalo Hawaiian Beach Bar, ideal for sipping frozen margaritas.

SPORTS

Singapore has facilities and locations for sports and athletics, but except for indoor pursuits, active visitors should take heed of the high humidity, timing workouts and other exhausting exercises for early morning or after sunset.

Indoors, Singapore offers more than 20 **bowling** alleys of more than 20 lanes. Some alleys are open 24-hours a day; most open about 9am and close an hour or two after midnight. The cost ranges from SGD2-4 per line (for information, contact the Singapore Tenpin Bowling Congress, Tel. 6440-7388). **Bicycling** and **mountain biking** have become increasingly popular, with rentals at Sentosa, East Coast Park, Pasir Ris, and on Pulau Ubin.

On the water, **canoeing** and **kayaking** are available at Sentosa, East Coast Park, and Changi Point, with single- and double-seaters for rent 9am–6pm daily. **Waterskiing** and **wakeboarding** are available at the Kallang River, where the world championships were once held. **Windsurfing** equipment and small **sailboats** can be rented through the Sea Sports Centre (Tel. 6449-5118), open 9:30am–6:30pm daily.

Scuba diving is offered by charter operators on Sentosa, with trips to Kusu, Sisters Islands, and other near points, but the waters around Singapore are not as rewarding to underwater explorers as those in Malaysia, Indonesia, and Thailand. The best **swimming** is on nearby islands, such as Sentosa and Kusu, but with such heavy shipping traffic in Singapore waters, most visitors prefer hotel swimming pools.

East Coast Park, located on the shoreline off the East Coast Parkway between Bedok and Marine Parade, is, like Sentosa Island,

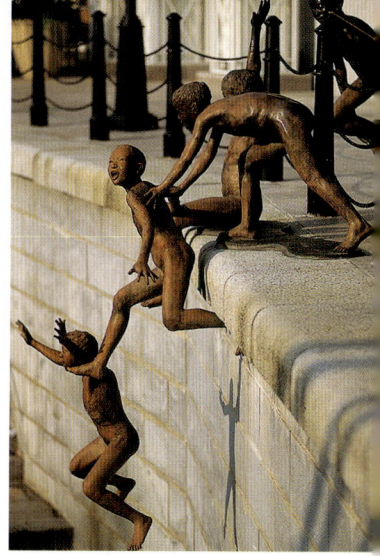

Riverbank sculpture located near to Cavenagh Bridge.

given over to fun and especially to sports. Here is a cluster of bowling alleys, bicycle rentals, and canoe, wakeboard, and windsurfing outlets for water sports enthusiasts. The East Coast Tennis Centre is nearby, as is the Laguna National Golf and Country Club.

Golf is extremely popular, and several of Singapore's golf courses are world-class, attracting such international tournaments as the Johnnie Walker Classic. There are 11 private golf courses that offer limited access to non-members and four public courses that have no restrictions on visitors. Greens fees range from as low as SGD10 at the 7-hole par-3 public Tanglin Golf Course (Minden Road; Tel. 6473-7236) to SGD150 for 18 holes at the private Laguna National Golf and Country Club (11 Laguna Golf Green; Tel. 6541-0289). These rates apply only to weekdays; weekend rates are often twice as high. Club rental is another SGD20-50. Private clubs prefer that players hire caddies, or at least a cart, and most have a dress code requiring collared polo shirts and proper golf shoes. Many clubs also require a handicap or proficiency-rating certificate. Courses are usually open from dawn to dusk (about 7am–7pm), but a few offer night golf under floodlights, as does the Orchid Country Club (1 Orchid Club Road; Tel. 6750-2112). The least expensive courses are the public links, but these are all 9 holes or less, and only one offers a full-sized par-36 layout (Seletar Base Golf Course, 244 Oxford Street, Seletar Base; Tel. 6481-8877).

Despite the heat and humidity, **hiking** is certainly one of Singapore's most attractive outdoor pursuits. The rain forests of the Bukit Timah Nature Reserve, the wetlands of the Sungei Buloh Nature Park (301 Neo Tiew Crescent), and the reservoir greenery of the MacRitchie Nature Trail (located off Thomson Road at the Central Catchment Nature Reserve) are the three most popular trekking areas.

Among the most popular spectator sports in Singapore are the **cricket**, **rugby**, or **field hockey** matches you might chance to see passing by the grassy Padang across from City Hall. Singapore also has its own **soccer** league, with local teams and sometimes international teams competing at Singapore's National Stadium. **Horseracing** under the stars at the Singapore Turf Club (1 Turf Club Avenue, near the Kranji MRT stop; Tel. 6879-1000) is the most popular spectator sport among Singapore's punters. Tourists (over 18 only) can watch the action from the air-conditioned Hibiscus Room (admission), where the dress code is smart casual. The cheap seats, two levels below and not air-conditioned, have

What to Do

the most lax dress code (shorts, singlets, slippers, and sandals without back straps are banned; Bermuda shorts and sleeveless T-shirts are permitted for women only). Swank is the word for this new racecourse (opened 1999), with a capacity of 30,000 betters and served by 500 "totalisator" counters. Races commence at 7:15pm Wednesdays, at 6pm Saturdays and some Sundays, with the program running until after 10pm. Numbers games (4-D) are also played three times nightly. The horses are imported, mostly from Australia, New Zealand, England, Ireland, and the US. This being Singapore, the Turf Club also offers its own food court (over 20 stalls), a public 9-hole golf course (Green Fairways), and a weekly lucky draw on all betting slips. The government's take on bets is 12 percent.

SINGAPORE FOR CHILDREN

Singapore is a perfect introduction to Asia for children. While there are exotic touches everywhere, and the cultures of China, Malaysia, and India are much in evidence, Singapore is also highly Westernized. English is widely spoken, familiar fast-food outlets are handy, safety is not a concern, and the hygiene is as good (or better) than at home. Best of all, Singapore is a family-

Close encounters with the Buddha of Bugis Village.

Singapore

oriented society, and families are encouraged to do things together. There's a wealth of attractions and entertainment options that are designed for visitors of all ages. Even many of the museums that display history and culture do so with children in mind, employing high-tech films and dioramas to tell their stories. Most attractions offer child discounts.

Sentosa Island is made for children, with its water park, beach activities, Underwater World oceanarium, and extensive array of amusement parks and rides. The **zoo** has a special area for younger children and the **Night Safari** provides something exciting for families to do together after nightfall. The **Jurong Bird Park** has highly entertaining shows. Many of the malls and shopping centers have video arcades and fountain shows. Singapore's dazzling array of festivals is lively enough to keep youngsters enthralled. The river cruises and island excursions via bumboats are also as much fun for kids as for adults. A number of other attractions are guaranteed to keep the kids — locals as well as visitors — entertained. The **Tiger Balm Gardens** provide a rare opportunity for foreign kids to mingle with local youngsters at one of Asia's oldest amusement parks, one designed with children in mind. East Coast Park has bicycle and in-line skating rentals, with safe riding trails.

Lakeside sculpture in the Singapore Botanic Gardens.

The **Escape Theme Park** (1 Pasir Ris Close; Tel. 6581-9135; admission; open Monday to Friday 10:30am–5pm; weekends 10am–10:30pm) is Singapore's largest theme park, with more than a dozen rides (including go-karts) and plenty of acrobats and jugglers performing daily. The **Singapore Discovery Centre** (510 Upper Jurong Road; Tel. 6792-6188; admission) is filled with interactive displays, virtual reality games, and even a shooting gallery. Its large-screen 3-D theater shows new films regularly (open Tuesday–Sunday 9am–7pm). The **Singapore Science Centre** (15 Science Centre Road; Tel. 6425-2500; admission), with 600 exhibits, has an aviation gallery and surround-sound theater (open Tuesday–Sunday 10am–6pm). Nearby is **Snow City** (Tel. 6560-0179; closed Mondays), where skiing and snowboarding take place indoors year round.

Temples are full of intriguing details.

FESTIVALS AND EVENTS

Singapore has a parade of **festivals** that occur in nearly every month of the year. With its multi-ethnic population, these festivals are a microcosm of world religion and culture. Many take place at temples, mosques, and religious shrines. Many also take place on dates determined by the lunar calendar or some other non-Western system, so it is vital to check with the Singapore Tourist Board, consult the Touristline (Tel. 1800-736-2000), or pick up the current festival brochure for exact dates from year to year.

CALENDAR OF EVENTS

January/February *Ponggal:* a four-day southern Hindu harvest festival, with conch-shell blowing and rice offerings, best seen at Sri Srinivasa Perumal Temple; *Chinese New Year:* fireworks, food, and dragon dances in the streets of Chinatown; *Singapore River Hong Bao:* cultural performances, dances, and fortune-telling at Marina Promenade, overlapping with Chinese New Year; *Chingay:* Singapore's largest street parade, with floats, stilt-walkers, lion dancers, and roller skaters, marking the end of the two-week Chinese New Year celebrations; *Thaipusam:* the city's most dramatic Hindu festival, a procession of devotees who pierce themselves with skewers and metal structures (*kavadis*), then undertake the 3-km (2-mile) pilgrimage from the Sri Srinivasa Perumal Temple to the Sri Thandayuthapani (Chettiar) Temple.

March/April *Hari Raya Haji:* this national Islamic holiday commemorates the *haj* (pilgrimage to Mecca) with prayers in mosques; *Qing Ming Festival:* family graves are swept clean (at the cemetery on Upper Thomson Road, for example), and temples (such as Kong Meng San Phor Kark See on Sin Ming Road) are jammed with families burning incense; *Birthday of Lao Zi:* followers celebrate the birthday of Lao Zi, founder of Daoism, and show the Way at a week-long display of performances and rituals at the Aljunied MRT station; *Singapore Food Festival:* an annual gourmet splash that runs throughout April with various special events; *Singapore International Film Festival:* 150 films from 35 countries; *Songkran:* Buddhist New Year Day festival, water-splashing and water pistols at Jalan Bukit Merah temple.

May/June/July *Vesak Day:* Buddhism's holiest day, commemorating the Buddha's entrance into Nirvana, marked by bird releases and nighttime candle procession at the Buddhist Lodge; *Singapore International Jazz Festival:* international and fringe concerts, in tandem with the *Singapore Airlines International Cup* horse race, the region's biggest, at

Kranji; *Singapore Dragon Boat Festival:* honoring Qu Yuan, a patriotic martyr who drowned, the Marina Bay regatta has international races and national championships, coinciding with the *Dumpling Festival* at Albert Mall; the *Great Singapore Sale:* big retail discounts for six weeks, including all of June; *Singapore Arts Festival:* top performers and fringe theater from East and West.

August/September *Festival of the Hungry Ghosts:* the spirits of the dead return in the 7th lunar month, attending street banquets, listening to *wayangs* (street operas) and shopping for arts and crafts; *National Day:* independence in 1965 is celebrated with massive patriotic parade and fireworks at the Padang; *Birthday of the Monkey God:* spirit mediums unsheathe their knives and monkey around at the Monkey God Temple on Seng Poh Road; *Navarathiri Festival:* nine nights devoted to three Hindu goddesses, with Indian music and a procession at Sri Mariamman Temple; *Mooncake Festival:* traditional mid-autumn festivities in Chinatown light up with large lantern festival in the Chinese Garden.

October/November/December *Deepavali:* the Festival of Lights ignites the streets and Hindu temples of Little India; *Thimithi Festival:* devotees fire-walk a 4-m (13-ft) carpet of burning coconut husks at the Sri Mariamman Temple; *Pilgrimage to Kusu Island:* Daoists pray for good fortune and fertility at Tua Pekong Temple on tiny "Turtle Island"; *Nine Emperor Gods Festival:* nine gods in nine days possess Daoist priests, with spirit messages and images paraded from the Kiu Ong Yiah Temple, Upper Serangoon Road; *Festival Light-Ups:* seasonal street and shop "light-ups" begin in Little India (Deepavali Light-Up), spread to Orchard Road (Christmas Light-Up) and Geylang Serai (Hari Raya Light-Up), and conclude in Chinatown (Lunar New Year Light-Up) as *Celebration Singapore* runs from November through February with Indian, Malaysian, Chinese, and Western celebrations.

EATING OUT

Singapore is the dining center of Asia, which makes it one of the premier dining destinations in the world. For food critics, gourmets, and hungry travelers inclined to favor Eastern over Western cuisines, Singapore is the best place on Earth to dine. The reasons are many. First, Singapore is situated (geographically, historically, and ethnically) on a culinary axis point where several of the world's top cuisines mix and mingle, from the great regional traditions of Chinese and Indian cooking to the more localized and unique cuisines of Malaysia and the Peranakans (Straits Chinese). Thai, Indonesian, Japanese, and Korean foods are also amply represented, as is first-rate fare from the West. Second, dining in Singapore is convenient, with good service the norm and English among the many languages in use everywhere. Third, restaurants are excellent values in Singapore, with hundreds of fine eating choices costing but a few dollars. Fourth, restaurants, even at the street level, are scrupulously clean and hygienic. Lastly, the dining is so varied and the food stalls, cafés, and restaurants so numerous (with over 20,000 places to dine), that travelers could not eat their way through Singapore even if they stayed several years.

The chief problem facing a traveler with a few days, or even a few weeks, is where to begin. One way to simplify this delicious dilemma is to make sure to sample each of Singapore's celebrated cuisines. Be sure to try out the various settings for meals, too, from hawker centers and quayside cafés to top hotel restaurants. Ask locals for tips, check out the latest local listings in Singapore's newspapers and magazines, or buy a Singapore dining guide from a local bookstore — but don't deliberate too long. If you see an interesting restaurant, take the plunge. Dining is so compet-

Eating Out

itive in Singapore that one can almost be guaranteed good meals and service, nearly anywhere and at nearly any hour. Singaporeans consider eating an even more important pursuit than shopping, so they pack thousands upon thousands of restaurants nearly around the clock. For dinners, especially on weekends, reservations are a must at establishments that accept them. Otherwise, join the lines; at Singapore cafés, restaurants, and food stalls. It is nearly always worth the wait.

Hawker Centers and Food Courts

Hawker centers are Singapore's answer to fast food. While street food and vendors' stalls pose hygienic threats to adventurous diners elsewhere in Asia, in Singapore the outdoor centers encircled by numerous vendors' counters are rigorously inspected for cleanliness. Best of all, meals are extremely inexpensive, with main courses costing just a few Singapore dollars. Pictures of each dish frequently decorate a food hawker's counter, with names in English, making ordering a snap. Some of these no-frill eateries are dedicated to a particular cuisine, but most offer a variety of Chinese, Malaysian, and Indian choices, cooked up fresh and on the

Hygiene standards are very high, even at hawker stalls.

Singapore

spot. Your meal is sometimes brought to you; other times you pick up your order on a tray. Utensils (including knives, forks, and spoons) are usually available at the counter. Find a table (which you may have to share) and make the most of the tempting dishes on offer.

Food courts are a fancier version of hawker centers, often located inside shopping malls. These are air-conditioned, with nicer tables and plates, perhaps, and the price is a little bit higher, but the same procedures apply. Order from the vendor of choice and your hot meal will quickly be ready. Tables may have numbers, so that the vendor can deliver your order as soon as it's ready. If there aren't custodians circulating, you should do the cleanup yourself.

Some of Singapore's most popular and crowded hawker centers are at Bugis Junction, along Orchard Road, in street markets and shopping arcades, and in Chinatown, while leading food courts can be found in nearly all shopping malls and at the quays along the Singapore River.

Chinese Cuisines

The majority of Singaporeans are ethnically Chinese, making the regional cuisines of China the most common offering. Chopsticks are the traditional eating utensil for these meals, although Western utensils can be supplied upon request.

The most common choices at Chinese restaurants and stalls are *dim sum* (small steamed pasta parcels and dumplings with a variety of fillings), chilli chicken, Peking duck, *popiah* (spring rolls with various fillings), Teochew porridge (made from rice), wonton soup, and *yong tau foo* (stuffed eggplant and bean curd, a Hakka specialty). Undoubtedly the single most popular dish is Hainanese chicken-rice (pieces of chicken steamed in stock and served over boiled white rice with a chilli-ginger sauce). Chicken-

Eating Out

rice is a staple at hawker centers, food courts, and most Chinese cafés and restaurants. *Hokkien fried mee* (fried noodles with prawns and pork) is almost a national dish here, as many Singaporean Chinese trace their ancestry to the Fujian (Hokkien) region of China. Teochew dishes originated in the Chaozhou (Chiu Chow) region of southeast China near Guangzhou (Canton), but the food is spicier than the better-known, related Cantonese cuisine. Steamboat is a common Teochow dish in Singapore, a hot pot of steaming oil delivered to the table into which raw vegetables, meats, and fish are dipped by the diner. Another Teochew specialty is iron Buddha tea, a dark tea as strong as coffee.

Singapore's restaurant scene is amply represented by more familiar regional cuisines, such as Cantonese and Szechuan fare. In fact, these are the two most popular Chinese choices. In Singapore, Chinese food is as fine and varied as in China itself; the vast and discerning local population of ethnic Chinese diners insures its quality and authenticity.

You are never very far from a good restaurant in Singapore, whatever your taste in food.

Singapore

> ### Tea with the Queen
>
> The perfect shopping and sightseeing break in bustling Singapore is a visit to a traditional teahouse. Singapore's best known and largest teahouse is Tea Chapter (9A Neil Road; Tel. 6226-3026; fax 6221-0604; web site <www.tea-chapter.com.sg>; open daily 11am–11pm, located between Chinatown and Tanjong Pagar). On 10 October 1989, Queen Elizabeth II and Prince Philip took their tea here in a private room upstairs overlooking the street. Visitors today can appreciate the pleasures of Chinese tea culture in the same room. The teas run the gamut, from greens to reds, but the service is traditional. First-timers are quickly versed in the art of tea. Water is heated at the table, the tea arrives in tiny packets, and scoops, tea clips, fragrance cups, saucers, and snacks complete the graceful setting. Guests can linger as long as they choose, savoring the atmosphere of a venerable refuge once the exclusive privilege of British royalty.

Malaysian Cuisine

Singapore's nearest neighbor, Malaysia, supplies some of the best food in the city. Heavily influenced by Indonesian cooking, Malaysian dishes tend to be hot and spicy, with generous doses of lemongrass, chillies, cloves, tamarind, and prawn paste. Coconut milk is also frequently added, tending to douse the fire.

The chief Malay dish is *satay*, skewers of meat that are spiced and marinated before barbecuing, which sets it apart from the Indonesian version. More difficult to find than strictly Chinese or Indian fare, Malay specialties are worth seeking out at the food stalls. At the Clarke Quay Satay Club, for example, you can purchase mutton, beef, or chicken satays served over *ketupat* (rice steamed in coconut leaves), accompanied by *sup kambing* (mutton soup) and *mamak mee goreng* (fried noodles with cabbage and mutton). Among other savory Malay offerings are *gado gado* (vegetable salad smothered in a coconut and peanut sauce, served with prawn crackers), *nasi goreng* (fried rice), *soto ayam* (spicy chicken soup), and *rojak* (a sweet and spicy mix of pineapple, cucumber, fried bean curd with prawn paste and peanuts).

Peranakan (Nonya) Cuisine

Nonya (which refers to the female member of a Peranakan or Straits-Chinese family of mixed Chinese and Malay heritage) is Singapore's most indigenous cuisine. Chinese and Malay ingredients and recipes have been transformed into some of Singapore's most delicious dishes, with Nonya restaurants proliferating in the Jalan Sultan and Tanjong Pagar areas. Coconut milk, shrimp paste (*belachan*), and chillies give Nonya dishes a unique flavor. Shrimp paste, chilli, and lime are pressed together to form an excellent condiment, *sambal belachan*. Dishes worth trying are *buah keluak* (chicken and black nuts in tamarind sauce), *laksa* (noodles in curry soup), *nonya kueh* (rice cakes with coconut and sugar), and *otak-otak* (minced fish flavored with lime and coconut,

Singapore is renowned for its fresh seafood dishes.

wrapped in banana leaves and charcoal-roasted) — a snack so zesty there are Peranakan restaurants serving almost nothing else.

Indian Cuisine

The Indian food in Singapore is on par with the best dishes prepared in India itself. The ingredients are fresh and the local Indian chefs know what they are doing, especially in preparing curries. In Singapore, diners are treated to the best of Northern and Southern Indian dishes, as well as creations that are uniquely Singaporean.

Northern Indian cuisine is mild and subtle, often employing yogurt, wheat breads, and *ghee* (clarified butter) rather than cooking oils. *Tandoori* (marinated meat or fish cooked in clay ovens) is the signature dish. In Singapore, the

Satay chicken and whole fish on a charcoal grill: typical food of an island that blends many culinary traditions.

Eating Out

local variations on traditional North Indian recipes have led to dishes like *mee goreng* (bean curd, lamb, and peas fried with thick noodles in a tomato sauce) and *sup kambing* (a mutton soup accompanied by French bread).

Southern Indian cuisine is spicier, and often less pricey. In Singapore, this cuisine is most often served in "banana-leaf" restaurants, where a banana leaf replaces the plate. Rice is ladled onto the big leaf, followed by mounds of chutneys, *dals* (pureed lentils), and curries. There are no utensils, and the meal is eaten by hand, with the rice pinched between one's fingers. For cleanup, use the sink that is a fixture on the wall of any banana-leaf restaurant.

Vegetarians will enjoy Singapore's Southern Indian foods, as many dishes are meatless. Little India has a number of inexpensive vegetarian cafés. Muslim Indian restaurants avoid pork, but they do use other meats, especially in dishes such as *biryani*, which has a basmati-rice base.

Indian cooking is known for its delicious breads, ranging from the unleavened, flat *chapati* to the fluffy *puri*, but in Singapore, one of the most popular Indian breads is known as *paratha*. Paratha (or *roti prata*) is a large, thin, folded pancake cooked on a hot griddle. When filled with mutton and egg, it becomes *murtabak*, a staple at Indian street stalls and hawker centers. Murtabak is the ideal Indian fast-food, and watching the murtabak man at work is far more entertaining than anything seen behind the counters of McDonald's.

Strangely enough, the best known Indian dish in Singapore is not Indian at all, but rather a regional invention, the fish-head curry. The fish head is usually that of a red snapper, boiled up in a spicy, complex curry and served eyeball-up on a banana leaf. During the annual Singapore Food Festival, there's usually a contest for the nation's best fish-head curry.

> ### Cooking Schools
> For those who want to learn the secrets of fine Asian cooking and unravel the mysteries of oriental herbs and spices, there are several top culinary schools that can oblige, with hands-on introductory courses conducted by top Singapore chefs, lasting from a day to several weeks. The at-sunrice academy (Fort Canning Centre, Singapore 179618; Tel. 6336-3307; fax 6336-9353; web site <www.at-sunrice.com>) offers two-week courses every summer for serious culinary students from abroad. The Raffles Culinary Academy (#02–17, Raffles Hotel Arcade, 1 Beach Road, Singapore 189673; Tel. 6412-1256; fax 6339-7013) is less formal, offering one-day classes on weekdays where noted chefs demonstrate the preparation of regional dishes. Guests, who are invited to participate, are rewarded with a complete gourmet meal.

Other Asian Cuisines

Asian cuisines are well represented by restaurants featuring Korean, Vietnamese, Japanese, and particularly Thai dishes. Thai recipes share many ingredients in common with Singapore's other great dishes, including chillies, coconut milk, tamarind, peanuts, noodles, and steamed rice, but these are shaped into distinctive creations. At the same time, the overlapping of so many intense Asian foods in tiny Singapore has created what might be called an Asian-fusion cuisine, blurring the distinctions between what is exclusively Cantonese or Malay, Indian or Peranakan in a given dish.

The confusion leads to some marvelous seafood dishes in Singapore, a port where fresh fish is easy to procure. The *al fresco* seafood restaurants along East Coast Parkway do a standing-in-line business nearly every

Eating Out

night, but it is difficult to tell if they are Chinese or Chinese-Malaysian or simply Singapore seafood restaurants. What's on the table is simply the fresh catch of the day, often perfectly prepared in any style you wish, with sauces of your choice. You can have your squid deep fried, your prawns in garlic, and your stingray barbecued. Singapore's signature seafood is its chilli crab, followed closely by the pepper crab. These are whole steamed crabs, only partially cracked, that are infused with chilli or pepper sauces or with the spicy sauce of your choice, tender and fiery.

Another unusual culinary tradition in Singapore is Chinese herbal cuisine. This food is Chinese in origin and medicinal in effect. Principles of yin and yang are followed in preparing each recipe, and herbs and spices believed to cure specific ailments season the food. Certain items are considered health-giving and curative in themselves, including rare varieties of mushrooms from mountain regions of China, which end up in Singapore's best herbal restaurants.

Delicious rice parcels cooked in coconut leaves.

Singapore

Western Cuisines

French, Italian, European, Mediterranean, Middle Eastern, and South American restaurants are scattered across Singapore, where Western food is quite popular, too. Top Western restaurants with foreign chefs are a staple at Singapore's international hotels, of course, but finding an excellent French restaurant with a French chef at the controls in downtown neighborhoods of Singapore is surprisingly easy. Colonial traditions continue as well, with high tea and tiffin a staple at Raffles, Goodwood Park, and a dozen more classy hotels. The American influence in eating is evident in the seemingly ubiquitous fast-food chains, from Pizza Hut to Starbucks. Not all American invaders are fast-food giants, however. Some of Singapore's best grills, delis, coffee shops and microbreweries are American transplants.

Some of Singapore's restaurants began combining Asian and Western ingredients and techniques even before the culi-

Dragon fruits: not to be missed on a visit to Singapore.

nary revolution of the US West Coast. East-West fusion food, dubbed New Asia-Singapore cuisine, places great emphasis on fresh, healthy, and simply cooked food and is well worth sampling at such establishments as Doc Cheng's and Club Chinois.

Strange Fruits

One of the delights of exploring Singapore on foot is the market, where all kinds of strange vegetables, spices, fruits, and sea creatures are available. Singapore's equatorial location means that tropical fruits head the list of exotic specimens not normally seen in Western supermarkets. The most notorious is the *durian*, known as the king of fruits by Singaporeans. Indeed, this spiny delight fetches royal prices when fresh, but to most outsiders, the smell of the durian is well beyond polite description. Public buildings in Singapore still display signs prohibiting the durian's very presence. Singaporeans and many Westerners do like the unusual flavor, however, and durian is used in a variety of foods, from desserts to flavored ice-cream bars.

Among the other fruits commonly found in Singapore's street markets are the *rambutan* (red and hairy in appearance), *mangosteen* (purple outside, white inside), *chiku* (brownish), *starfruit* (aptly named for its shape), and the dramatically red and white *dragon fruit*, whose mild taste is neither smoky nor fiery but tastes of kiwi fruit.

Drinks and Desserts

Singapore serves some superb drinks at its hawker centers, food courts, and ethnic restaurants. Ginger tea, a staple of Indian drinks vendors at hawker centres and coffee shops, is a noble contender to the lattes of Starbucks and other coffee invaders. An even more direct contender is *kopi tarek*, the

Singapore

"pulled coffee" that is poured by the maker from cup to pitcher and back again in a cascading performance. Little India abounds with pulled coffee stalls. The same stunt is pulled with condensed milk and tea to produce *teh tarek*, noted for its delicious foam.

In markets and food courts, try the freshly squeezed juices; they're cheaper and far healthier than canned sodas. Lime and mango can be quite refreshing. Locals love *chendol*, coconut milk mixed with brown sugar, red beans, and green starch strips. The local beer is Tiger, a refreshing pilsner-style beer. Green teas are still favored by many Singaporean Chinese, served hot. Iced tea can be found in restaurants, but it's not a local favorite. The trendiest development in drinks is bubble tea (also called pearl tea), an import from Taiwan. At a typical bubble teahouse, the teas are laced with tapioca pearls, shaken until they bubble, then flavored with fruit syrups, sugar, milk, ice cream — or whatever the flavor of the month happens to be.

Refreshing local desserts, aimed at cooling the day's heat, are *es delima*, water chestnuts in coconut milk and sago; *bo-bo cha cha*, crushed ice with palm sugar and sweet yam; and the ubiquitous *ice kachang* (or *ais kacang*), a huge cone of shaved ice festooned with corn, red beans, jelly cubes, evaporated milk, and colored syrups.

'Pulled coffee' ends up with a delicious sweet foam.

HANDY TRAVEL TIPS
An A–Z Summary of Practical Information

- **A** Accommodation 110
  Airport 110

- **B** Budgeting for Your Trip 111

- **C** Car Rental 112
  Climate 113
  Clothing 113
  Complaints 113
  Crime and Safety 114
  Customs and Entry Requirements 114

- **D** Driving 115

- **E** Electricity 117
  Embassies, Consulates and High Commissions 117
  Emergencies 118

- **G** Gay and Lesbian Travelers 118
  Getting to Singapore 118
  Guides and Tours 119

- **H** Health and Medical Care 120
  Holidays 120

- **L** Language 121
  Laundry 121

- **M** Maps 122
  Media 122
  Money 123

- **O** Open Hours 123

- **P** Police 124
  Post Offices 124
  Public Transportation 124

- **R** Religion 126

- **T** Telephone 126
  Tickets 127
  Time Zones 127
  Tipping 127
  Toilets 128
  Tourist Information 128

- **W** Water 129
  Web Sites 129
  Weights and Measures 130

- **Y** Youth Hostels 130

Singapore

ACCOMMODATION

There are **hotels** for every budget in Singapore. Major American and international hotel chains are well represented. Most hotels are concentrated in the Civic District (Raffles City, Marina Square areas), on or near Orchard Road, and along the Singapore River. The Singapore Hotel Association's website, <www.stayinginsingapore.com>, offers online hotel reservations. If you arrive without hotel reservations, the Singapore Hotel Association counters at the Changi Airport can arrange bookings. Pensions, hostels, and Bed & Breakfast accommodations are few, but there are lots of budget hotels (many with air-conditioning). Travel agents, package travel services, and travel web sites offer accommodation deals with substantial savings.

AIRPORT

Singapore Changi Airport (Tel. 6542-4422; web site <www.changi.airport.sg>) is frequently rated the best in the world in leading travel publications. Disembarking passengers will discover why, as the march (assisted by moving sidewalks) through customs, immigration, and baggage claim usually takes just a matter of minutes. There are two large terminals with a third under construction. Clean, modern facilities include full-service banks, currency exchange counters, communication centers with telephone, fax, telegraph, copiers, and Internet, post offices, free luggage trolleys, left luggage storage, and duty-free shops. There are also hotel and car-rental desks, nurseries, clinics, and restaurant and bar areas serving a wide range of international foods and drinks. Taxis, shuttle vans (the Maxicab), and city buses are always available at terminal entrances (a 10-mile/16-km journey to downtown).

Arrive two hours early for departing flights. Leaving Singapore, all passengers must pay an airport departure tax (SGD15), but if this

Travel Tips

is not incorporated in your air ticket, you are not required to pay it upon check-in. Transit passengers waiting a minimum of five hours may qualify for free city tours (check at the New Asia-Singapore Tour counter). A transit hotel is available in both terminals, renting rooms inexpensively in six-hour increments (Tel. 6542-8122; fax 6542-6122; <www.airport-hotel.com.sg>). Showers, saunas, and gym facilities are also available for hire for travelers wishing to freshen up during a stopover. The airport and most facilities are open daily 7am-11pm. The flight information hotline (toll-free in Singapore only) is Tel. 1800-542-4422.

B

BUDGETING FOR YOUR TRIP

Singapore has the second-highest standard of living in Asia (behind Japan), so expect many prices to be only slightly below those in North America and Northern Europe. Food and transportation can be bargains. **Meals** at hawker centers and food courts can be as little as SGD5. **Subway (MRT)** fares average between SGD1 and SGD2. Taxis from the airport are SGD15-25; taxi trips around town are considerably less, often as little as SGD6; and city buses are still cheaper (SGD1-2). **Hotels** run the gamut, from under SGD39 per person for budget choices to over SGD500 for top accommodations. Private city **tours** are priced at SGD25-100 and up.

Entrance fees are reasonable (SGD2-10), but **entertainment** costs (for performances, nightclubs, hotel night spots, bar and lounge drinks) can be as high as in Western capitals. Budget travelers can certainly visit Singapore cheaply, but Thailand, Malaysia, Indonesia, and other nearby Southeast Asian destinations offer much lower prices on nearly everything. Singapore offers convenience, cleanliness, efficiency, superb meals, and some great attractions, but it is not the bargain basement of Asia.

C

CAR RENTAL

Car rental is seldom necessary in Singapore, since it is compact and served by excellent and inexpensive forms of public transportation, but major car rental companies are in operation all over the island, including at the airport and downtown in the hotel districts. The Singapore government, in a concerted effort to reduce traffic congestion, has made car rental and use, especially in the central business district, an expensive and sometimes complicated affair. Rates for the smallest cars start at around SGD150 per day (including insurance, CWD, and unlimited mileage). Rental cars can be taken into Malaysia, but surcharges and gasoline restrictions apply (the tank must be full upon leaving Singapore). A valid driver's license from your country of residence or a valid International Driving License is required, as is a major credit card. Some companies rent cars only to those over 21 and under 60. Despite the fact that oil refineries engulf Singapore's harbors, gasoline prices are higher than in some European countries — and up to three times higher than in the US.

Major car rental companies in Singapore include:

Avis: Tel. 6737-1668 in Singapore, Tel. 800/321-3712 in the US; <www.avis.com>

Budget: Tel. 6742-0119 in Singapore, Tel. 800/935-6878 in the US; <www.budgetrentacar.com>

Hertz: Tel. 1800-734-4646 in Singapore, Tel. 800/654-3011 in the US; <www.hertz.com>

National: Tel. 6737-1668 in Singapore, Tel. 800/227-7368 in the US; <www.nationalcar.com>

Sintat: Tel. 6295-2211.

Avis and Sintat rent cars at the Changi Airport.

Hotels can often arrange for a car and driver; chauffeur-driven luxury cars can cost SGD50 per hour and up.

Travel Tips

CLIMATE

Singapore's tropical climate is fairly uniform, as are the hours of sunrise and sunset (6:30-7 am, 6:30-7pm), due to its location just 85 miles (135 km) north of the equator. Rainfall is heaviest from November through January. Humidity is routinely very high year-round, (averaging about 85 percent). Expect daytime temperatures to soar near the average maximum of 88°F (31°C) in the afternoon and night-time lows to dip to near the average minimum of 75°F (24°C) just before sunrise. The lowest temperature ever recorded in Singapore was 68.9°F (19.4° C). Annual rainfall averages 92 inches (2,337 mm), with sudden but brief downpours common. The weather forecast is available by phone, Tel. 6542-7788.

CLOTHING

The island's dress code is casual but neat. Short-sleeved cotton sportswear is acceptable almost everywhere. Even businesspeople seldom wear suits or jackets. Some tourists wear shorts, but Singapore residents seldom do. Mosques require that arms and legs be fully covered (by long-sleeved shirts, long pants and long skirts or sarongs) to enter. Sikh temples require a head covering, as do synagogues for males. Raincoats are hardly necessary, although a light sweater or wrap is sometimes required in the evening. Umbrellas are handy in a downpour. Hats and sunscreen can protect against the ravages of the fierce tropical sun. Comfortable walking shoes, sandals, and sunglasses are useful for getting around.

COMPLAINTS

Unsatisfactory retail practices can be reported to the Retail Promotion Centre, Blk 528, Ang Mo Kio Ave 10, #02-2387 (Tel. 6450-2114; fax 6458-6393). Redress from retailers can be secured on short notice, with judgments rendered immediately, at the Small Claims Tribunal, located at #05-00 Apollo Centre, No. 2 Havelock Road (Tel. 6435-5937/6553-5383; fax 6435-5994) and at #03-265 Block 50 Marine Terrace (Tel. 6241-3575; fax 6241-8938). There is

Singapore

also a free dispute resolution service online at <www.e-adr.org.sg>. Touts are illegal in Singapore. Report them, as well as unscrupulous taxi drivers and others, to your hotel desk or the Singapore Tourism Board (Tourism Court, 1 Orchard Spring Lane; Tel. 6736-6622; fax 6736-9423; <www.newasia-singapore.com>).

CRIME and SAFETY

Singapore has the lowest crime rate in Southeast Asia, but pickpockets and purse snatchers do operate, usually around neighborhood markets, even though the penalty for pickpocketing is three years in jail and four strokes of the cane. Crime is also very low in hotels, which have discreet security forces, but use the hotel safety box or room safe for valuables. Report stolen property and other crimes immediately to your hotel and the Tanglin Police Station, 17 Napier Road (Tel. 6733-0000).

Remember that Singapore has strict laws covering infractions that might be considered minor elsewhere. Littering can result in a SGD1,000 fine for first-time offenders. Smoking is banned in public places, including restaurants, and buses and taxis; the fine is SGD1,000. The chewing of gum is not banned, but the sale of chewing gum is subject to a SGD2,000 fine.

Drug offenses are dealt with harshly in Singapore. The death penalty is mandatory for those convicted of trafficking, manufacturing, importing, or exporting 15g of heroin, 30g of cocaine, 30g of morphine, 500g of cannabis, 200g of cannabis resin, or 1.2kg of opium. Possession of these quantities is considered *prima facie* evidence of drug trafficking. Those convicted of drug consumption face maximum prison terms of 10 years and a fine of up to SGD20,000. Singapore is not the place to bring, buy, or use illegal drugs.

CUSTOMS and ENTRY REQUIREMENTS

Citizens of Australia, New Zealand, South Africa, the United Kingdom, the Republic of Ireland, Canada, and the US, as well as of the Commonwealth, Western Europe, and South America, need

Travel Tips

only a valid passport (good for six months) to enter Singapore for a tourist or business visit lasting up to 30 days. Tourists, however, should also carry onward/return tickets to their next destination and sufficient funds for their stay in Singapore. For longer stays, apply to the Singapore Immigration & Registration office (10 Kallang Road) or call the hotline (Tel. 6391-6100) upon arrival. Vaccination certificates are required only of passengers who arrive from cholera- or yellow fever-infected areas. An immigration card, supplied before arrival, must be filled out and kept with the passport for surrender upon departure.

There is no limit on the amount of currency or traveler's checks you can bring into Singapore. Customs limitations for personal consumption apply to certain items, including spirits (1 liter), wine or port (1 liter), and beer, stout or ale (1 liter). There are no concessions on cigarettes and other tobacco products (in line with the government's campaign to discourage smoking). Travelers with medicines must bring prescriptions authorizing their use. Prohibited items include controlled drugs and psychotropic substances, weapons, ammunition, endangered species and their by-products, firecrackers, seditious and treasonable materials, and obscene (pornographic) articles, publications, video tapes, and software. A complete list of prohibited, restricted, and dutiable goods is available through the Customs Duty Officer, Singapore Changi Airport (Tel. 6542-7058 or 6543-0755).

Lost or stolen passports should be reported to the police; then to Singapore Immigration (10 Kallang Road; Tel. 6391-6100), where temporary passports are issued, and finally to your embassy.

D

DRIVING

If you decide to drive in Singapore, note that you must drive on the left, overtake on the right, and fully yield to pedestrians at

Singapore

designated crossing points. A valid driver's license or International Driving License is required. Speed limits are 50km/h (30mph) in residential areas, 80–90km/h (40–50mph) on expressways. Singapore roads are in excellent condition and signposted in English. Speed cameras are installed throughout the island. Bus lanes or lanes with unbroken yellow lines can only be used by buses during rush hours (Monday–Friday 7:30–9:30am, 4:30–7pm; Saturday 7:30–9:30am, 11:30am–2pm).

All vehicles entering the Central Business District (CBD) from 7:30am to 7pm are required to pay an Electronic Pricing Scheme (ERP) toll. All vehicles are installed with an In-Vehicle Unit (IU) and a CashCard (stored value card) which automatically deducts the toll from the CashCard each time the vehicle passes through an ERP gantry. Temporary IU devices are available. The toll varies with the time of day and entry point. The ERP is not in operation at New Year, Lunar New Year, Hari Raya Puasa, Deepavali, and Christmas. There are tolls for using the Causeway and Second Link bridges that connect Singapore and Malaysia.

Driving information is available from Traffic Watch (toll-free 1800-222-2233), the Automobile Association of Singapore (Tel. 6737-2444), and the ERP hotline (toll-free 1800-553-5226). The Automobile Association of Singapore emergency road service operates 24-hours a day (Tel. 6748-9911). The traffic police can be contacted at Tel. 6547-0000.

At public car parks and for on-street parking, a pre-paid parking coupon must be displayed indicating the date and time of arrival. These parking coupons are sold at special kiosks, petrol stations, post offices, and shopping centers and shops throughout the city. Paid parking is also available at most shopping centers and some public buildings. Signs indicate the rates, and coupons can be bought from machines to display on the dashboard.

Gasoline (petrol) is sold by the liter (one US gallon equals 3.8 liters; one imperial gallon equals 4.5 liters).

Travel Tips

Fluid measures

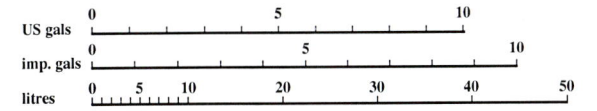

(US gals, imp. gals, litres conversion scales)

Distance

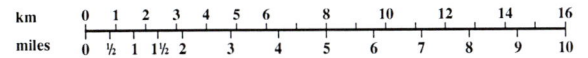

(km, miles conversion scales)

E

ELECTRICITY
Singapore's voltage is 220–240 A.C., 50 Hertz. Most hotels provide a transformer to convert to 110–120 A.C., 60 Hertz. Outlets require plugs with two round large prongs or the three-pronged square type.

EMBASSIES, CONSULATES and HIGH COMMISSIONS
Foreign missions and embassies are generally open Monday to Friday, 9am to 5pm, although some work shorter hours.

Australia: High Commission, 25 Napier Road, Tel. 6836-4100.

Canada: High Commission, 80 Anson Road, Tel. 6325-3200.

Ireland: Embassy, 298 Tiong Bahru Road, Tel. 6276-8935.

New Zealand: High Commission, 391A Orchard Road, Tel. 6235-9966.

South Africa: Embassy, North Bridge and Bras Basah Roads, Tel. 6339-3319.

UK: High Commission, 100 Tanglin Road, Tel. 6473-9333.

US: Embassy, 27 Napier Road, Tel. 6476-9100.

Singapore

EMERGENCIES
If you are in a hotel, call the front desk, operator, or hotel security. General emergency telephone numbers are:

Police	**999**
Ambulance	**995**
Fire	**995**

G

GAY and LESBIAN TRAVELERS
Homosexual activity is illegal in Singapore. Prison sentences run from 10 years to life. This said, there is a discreet homosexual scene, with entertainment venues, including transvestite shows, centered in the vicinity of Syed Alwi, Rowell, and Desker roads in Little India and, to a very limited extent, Bugis Street.

GETTING TO SINGAPORE
By air: Singapore is served by about 70 international airlines, representing more than 50 countries. As a major Asian hub, Singapore's Changi Airport is a superb stopover. Relatively inexpensive air tickets to nearby countries can be purchased through hundreds of travel agents in Singapore (although even cheaper prices can often be had in Malaysia, just across the Causeway Bridge from Singapore). Consolidator tickets, advanced tickets, circle-Pacific tickets, and round-the-world tickets can cut the cost of reaching Singapore, but not the hours it takes to get from America or Europe. High season tickets (June to September and December to January, from Europe and North America; December to January from Australia and New Zealand) are the most expensive.

Singapore Airlines, the national air carrier, is frequently rated the world's best airline. It offers non-stop and one-stop flights to and from many cities, including Vancouver in Canada; Los Angeles, San Francisco, and Chicago in the US; Adelaide, Brisbane, Melbourne, Perth, and Sydney in Australia; Auckland and Christchurch in New

Travel Tips

Zealand; London and Manchester in the UK; and Durban and Johannesburg in South Africa (as well as to and from Copenhagen, Frankfurt, Madrid, Paris, Rome, and Zurich). Singapore Airlines has offices in all the countries it serves, including the US (Tel. 800-742-3333), the UK (Tel. 020-8747-0007), Canada (Tel. 800-387-0038), Ireland (Tel. 01-671-0722), Australia (Tel. 02-9236-0111), New Zealand (Tel. 09-379-3209), South Africa (Tel. 011-880-8560), and in Singapore itself (Paragon Building, 290 Orchard Road; Tel. 6223-8888; web site <www.singaporeair.com.sg>). Singapore Airlines provides for early check-in (up to 48 hours in advance) at its Singapore office.

Singapore is also served by many North American airlines, including United, Northwest, Delta, and Canadian Airlines; by European airlines, including British Airways, Finnair, KLM, Lauda Air, Lufthansa, and Swiss Air; by Asian airlines, including Cathay Pacific, Garuda, Japan Air Lines, Korean Airlines, Malaysian Airlines, and Thai Airways; and by Qantas Airlines and Air New Zealand.

By rail: Visitors can also enter and leave Singapore via bus or rail through Malaysia. Five trains a day, all operated by Keretapi Tanah Melayu Berhard (KTMB), connect Singapore to Kuala Lumpur and other west coast and central Malaysian cities. A daily International Express Train connects Singapore to Thailand, as does the ultra-upscale Eastern & Orient Express (Tel. 6392-3500 in Singapore, 800-524-2420 in US), which takes 41 hours to make the Bangkok–Singapore run, with a tour of Penang thrown in for good measure. The Singapore Railway Station is on Keppel Road, a 20 minute walk from the Tanjong Pagar MRT station (Tel. 6224-5165).

GUIDES and TOURS

Various private and group tours are offered by Singapore tour companies. These can be booked directly or through hotel tour desks. Use guides licensed and trained by the Singapore Tourism

Singapore

Board (STB). There are city tours, historic tours, tours geared to specific attractions, evening tours, and harbor and river tours, as well as specialized tours focusing on food, farming, Chinese opera, feng shui, and horseracing. Leading tour operators include the award-winning Holiday Tours (Tel. 6738-2622) and Singapore Sightseeing Tour East (Tel. 6332-3755). Geraldine Lowe-Ismail gives authoritative private walking tours, including historical tours of Little India and Chinatown, architectural tours, gastronomical tours, and botanical tours, conducted in English or Italian (06-08 Orchard Court, 27 Oxley Road; Tel/fax. 6737-5250).

H

HEALTH and MEDICAL CARE

Singapore has no free medical care, and medical evacuation is very expensive, so be sure that you are covered by your travel insurance. Most hotels have doctors on call around the clock. Singapore's medical facilities are the finest in Asia. The Raffles SurgiCentre (182 Clemenceau Avenue; Tel. 6334-3337) is a 24-hour clinic, and the Singapore General Hospital on Outram Road (Tel. 6222-3322 or 6321-4113) is also always open. For ambulance service, dial 995. Pharmacies are open 9am to 6pm, sometimes later, but it is wise to travel with your own prescriptions and medications. Drink plenty of liquids to avoid heat exhaustion, and use sunscreen.

HOLIDAYS

The following state and national holidays are observed throughout Singapore. Banks and government offices are closed on these dates, as are some shops and malls. When a religious holiday falls on a Sunday, the following Monday is usually a national holiday.

New Year's Day	1 January
Chinese New Year	first day of first lunar month; usually in January or February

Travel Tips

Hari Raya Haji	Muslim pilgrimage celebration; date changes annually
Good Friday	Friday before Easter Sunday; usually in March or April
Labor Day	1 May
Vesak Day	Buddha's birthday, 8th day of the 4th lunar month; usually in May or June
National Day	9 August
Deepavali	Hindu festival; usually in October/November
Hari Raya Puasa	last day of Ramadan, 9th month of the Islamic calendar; date changes annually
Christmas	25 December

L

LANGUAGE

Singapore has four official languages: English (the language of administration), Chinese (Mandarin), Tamil, and Malay. English is widely spoken, making travel by English-speaking tourists a delight. Malay, designated as the National Language, is spoken by only 15 percent of the population, but understood by many Singaporeans. Mandarin Chinese is being pushed by the government as the preferred Chinese language, but Singapore's ethnic Chinese majority speaks one or more of the southern languages as well, including Hokkien, Teochew, Cantonese, Hainanese, Hakka, and Foochow. Singapore's ethnic Indians speak Tamil, but many also speak Telugu, Punjabi, Hindi, Bengali, and other regional languages. English serves as the island's lingua franca, although the government is attempting to discourage the use of a widespread local form of pidgin known as Singlish, or Singaporean English.

LAUNDRY

Large hotels and resorts usually have same-day laundry and dry cleaning services (expensive), although some hotels, including the

Singapore

Traders Hotel, provide self-serve washers and dryers. Commercial dry cleaning and laundries abound, as do coin-operated laundromats.

M

MAPS

Free city maps are available at most hotels and at travel information centers. The free monthly *Singapore Official Guide* and the *Where Singapore* and *This Week Singapore* magazines also contain maps. Bus/MRT maps are available in subway stations. The Singapore map from Periplus is quite detailed, and it can be purchased at bookstores in Singapore and overseas.

MEDIA

Of the eight major daily newspapers published in Singapore, four are in English, led by the *Straits Times*, which covers local, regional, and international news. Local magazines in English include *I-S*, *Where Singapore*, and *Eight Days*, all of which cover entertainment, attractions, and shopping; and *The Food Paper* and *Wine and Dine*, which concentrate on dining. International newspapers and magazines are available at bookstores, newsstands, shopping centers, and hotel kiosks. Some publications are subject to government-controlled circulation quotas. Magazines such as *Playboy* are banned, as are any publications with articles deemed harmful or offensive to Singapore.

Cable and satellite TV broadcasts, with CNN, BBC, MTV, NHK, ESPN and other common channels, are widely available in hotels, but their programs are monitored to filter out objectionable material. Local TV stations, operated by a government consortium, can be seen on Channels 5, 8, and 12. Channel 5 is mostly broadcast in English, Channel 8 mostly in Chinese and Tamil, and Channel 12 is a multi-lingual arts and culture station. Several stations from Malaysia are also received in Singapore.

Four of the local radio stations broadcast in English. BBC World News Service is available on short-wave receivers.

Travel Tips

MONEY

Currency. The Singapore dollar (abbreviated SGD) is divided into 100 cents, with coins of 1, 5, 10, 20, 50 cents and SGD1. Bills in common circulation are SGD1, SGD5, SGD10, SGD20, SDG50, SGD100, SGD500, SGD1,000, and SGD10,000.

Currency exchange. Money changing services are available at the Changi Airport and at most banks, hotels, and shopping complexes. Licensed money changers usually give slightly better rates than banks; hotels give the worst rates. Avoid unlicensed money changers. The exchange rates at the airport are on par with those at downtown banks.

Credit cards. Major credit cards are widely accepted by Singapore's restaurants, hotels, shops, travel agencies, and taxis.

Traveler's checks. Traveler's checks are easy to exchange for local currency and are accepted at many stores, restaurants, and hotels.

Report lost or stolen credit cards immediately to the police (Tel. 6733-0000). In Singapore, you can call American Express (Tel. 6299-8133), Diner's Club (Tel. 6294-4222), or Mastercard and Visa (Tel. 1800-345-1345) for replacements.

ATMs. Automated teller machines are everywhere (at banks, shopping malls, and many hotels). The Cirrus, PLUS, and Star system machines work in Singapore just as they do at home. Be sure you have your PIN number with you when you travel. Screen instructions are in English.

O

OPEN HOURS

Museums and tourist attractions have varying hours, but many open about 9:30am and close at 4 or 5pm; some are closed at least one day a week. Banks are usually open Monday to Friday 9:30am to 3pm, Saturdays 9:30am to 12:30pm (but Saturday hours can vary). Government offices operate Monday to Friday 8am to 6pm; some are

Singapore

open on Saturday. Many restaurants keep long hours, from dawn to midnight daily. Department stores and shopping centers are generally open daily from 10am to 9pm.

P

POLICE
To report a crime to the Singapore police, dial 999, or visit the Tanglin Police Station, 17 Napier Road (near Orchard Road).

POST OFFICES
Letters and postcards can be dropped off at hotel front desks, which often sell postage. Branches of the Singapore Post are open Monday to Friday 8:30am to 5pm. The Singapore Post branch at #04–15 Takashimaya, Ngee Ann City, 391 Orchard Road (Tel. 6738-6899) is open Monday to Friday 8:30am to 6pm, Saturday 9:30am to 2pm. The General Post Office (10 Eunos Road, Paya Lebar MRT station) is open Monday to Friday 8am to 10pm, Saturday 8am to 6pm, Sunday 10am to 4pm. The Changi Airport Post Office is open daily 8am to 8pm. For post office inquiries and locations, dial 1605. Airborne Express, DHL, FedEx, TNT, and UPS provide courier services as well.

PUBLIC TRANSPORTATION
Buses. Singapore has a highly efficient public bus system. Fares are SGD0.60 to SGD1.20 for non-air-conditioned buses, SGD0.70 to SGD1.50 for air-conditioned buses. Ask the driver for the fare to your destination; exact change is required. Buses operate daily 6am to midnight. An ez-link farecard (stored value transportation card) makes paying easier and is valid on all buses and the MRT subway. Another option is the Tourist Day Ticket, allowing 12 rides a day, regardless of distance. These cards can be purchased at any TransitLink office, located in most MRT stations, bus interchange booths, and many shopping centers and

Travel Tips

hotels. A pocket-sized transportation map, the TransitLink Guide, can also be purchased at these outlets.

The Singapore Trolley (Tel. 6339-6833), a tram bus, cruises past Orchard Road, the Civic District, the Singapore River, Raffles Hotel, Clarke Quay, and Suntec City daily. Unlimited daily tickets, including a riverboat tour, can be purchased from the trolley driver or at some hotels.

Subway (MRT). Singapore's Mass Rapid Transit (MRT) system is very efficient and simple to use. It operates from 6am to midnight daily, with trains arriving every 3 to 8 minutes. Single trip tickets start at SGD0.80, but stored value cards can be purchased at ticket windows. Rush hours should be avoided. For information, Tel. 1800-336-8900, Monday to Friday.

Trishaws. These modern rickshaws can make for an interesting tour, but be sure to agree on the full fare before boarding. Some tour operators offer city tours by trishaw.

Taxis. Singapore's 15,000 taxis are air-conditioned, comfortable, and highly efficient. Most of the drivers are exceptionally friendly and helpful, although a few can be a bit gruff. You can flag down a taxi in the street, but it is best to wait at a taxi stand at hotels, MRT stations, near bus stops, and at shopping centers. All taxis are metered; most accept credit cards. Basic fares are SGD2.40–3.20 for the first km, SGD0.10 for each 200–225m thereafter, with extra charges for waiting time. A variety of surcharges are thrown in for midnight to 6am trips (50 percent is added to the meter fare), peak period travel, travel into restricted downtown zones, advanced booking, and airport travel. Even with all the surcharges, taxi rides are inexpensive. The three major taxi companies are CityCab (Tel. 6552-2222), Comfort (Tel. 6552-1111), and TIBS (Tel. 6555-8888).

Airport shuttle (MaxiCab). Provided by CityCab, the 6-seat MaxiCab (with luggage storage and wheelchair accessibility) runs daily 9am to 11pm every 15 to 30 minutes from Changi Airport to

Singapore

most of the hotels within the city. Inexpensive tickets can be booked at airport shuttle counters in the airport terminals. The driver accepts cash or credit cards. Tel. 6553-3880.

R

RELIGION

Singapore's major religions are Buddhism (42.5%), Islam (14.9%), Christianity (14.6%), Daoism (8.5%), and Hinduism (4.0%). Other religions, including Judaism, account for 0.6%, with 14.8% of the population reporting no religious affiliation. Nearly every Christian denomination has a church in Singapore. Many residents happily worship at the shrines of other religions.

T

TELEPHONE

The country code for Singapore is 65. International telephone rates are among the lowest in the world. International calls to Singapore are made by dialing the international access code for the originating country, followed by Singapore's country code (65) and the seven-digit local number. International calls from Singapore are made by dialing the international access code (001, 013 or 019) followed by the country code, area code (minus the initial zero), and local number.

Most telephones in Singapore operate using phone cards (stored value cards) purchased from stores or post offices. International calling cards can be used from any phone; simply dial the calling card's access number for Singapore and follow the instructions. Both phone cards and international calling cards can be purchased in Singapore as well. Discount calling plans from your home country are also economical to use; again, dial your plan's toll-free access number to reach one of the plan's operators and follow instructions. Some hotels block such plans or levy surcharges. Hotels are usually the most expensive locations from which to place international calls.

Travel Tips

The Home Country Direct Service allows you to contact an operator in your home country from any pay phone and most hotel phones; the call is billed to your home phone or telephone credit card.

Local calls in Singapore cost SGD0.10 for three minutes from public phones. No area codes are used within Singapore. Dial 100 for local call assistance; dial 104 for overseas call assistance.

TICKETS

Tickets to performing arts and athletic events can be booked by phone or in person (and paid for in both cases by credit card) through SISTIC (Tel. 6348-5555) or Ticketcharge (Tel. 6296-2929). SISTIC outlets are located at 43 Pekin Street (Far East Square), 2 Stamford Road (Raffles City), and 6 Scotts Road (Scotts Shopping Centre). Ticketcharge outlets are located at 176 Orchard Road (Centrepoint) and 435 Orchard Road (Wisma Atria).

TIME ZONES

Singapore time is GMT + 8 hours year-round. Thus, in the winter, when it is 6pm in Singapore it is 2am (16 hours earlier) in Los Angeles and Vancouver, 5am (13 hours earlier) in New York and Toronto, 10 am (8 hours earlier) in London and Dublin, noon (6 hours earlier) in Johannesburg, 8pm (2 hours later) in Sydney, and 10pm (4 hours later) in Auckland. Although the clock is advanced one hour in summer in some countries (such as the US), it stays the same in Singapore. For the time of day in Singapore, Tel. 1711.

TIPPING

Tipping is not the normal practice in Singapore. It is banned at the Changi Airport and discouraged in many hotels and restaurants, where a 10% service charge is routinely added to bills. If no service charge is included in a dining bill, a 10% tip is expected (except at hawker centers and food courts). Tour guides and drivers appreciate tips (5 to 10%) as well. Very small tips

Singapore

(SGD1–2) can be paid to taxi drivers, hairdressers, doormen, porters, and hotel housekeeping staff.

TOILETS

Singapore's public restrooms, almost universally clean, are regularly inspected by health department officials. There's sometimes a small charge for their use, and there's a hefty fine for not flushing the toilets after use (although many now flush automatically). Shopping centers, malls, restaurants, hotel lobbies, and most tourist attractions provide restrooms.

TOURIST INFORMATION

The Singapore Tourism Board (STB) is a superb organization, offering mountains of free and helpful literature to visitors. Their website is <www.newasia-singapore.com>.

STB offices abroad include:

Australia: Singapore Tourism Board, Level II, AWA Building, 47 York Street, Sydney NSW 2000; Tel. (61-2) 9290-2888 or 9290-2882; fax (61-2) 9290-2555. Singapore Tourism Board, Representative Office, Level 1, 235 Queen Street, Melbourne VIC 3000; Tel. (61-3) 9606-0222; fax (61-3) 9606-0322. Singapore Tourism Board, c/o Sandra Devahasdin PR, Unit 2, 226 James Street, Perth WA 6000; Tel. (61-08) 9228-8166; fax (61-08) 9228-8290.

Canada: Singapore Tourism Board, 2 Bloor Street West, Suite 404, Toronto, Ontario M4W 3E2; Tel. (416) 363-8898; fax (416) 363-5752.

New Zealand: Singapore Tourism Board, Representative Office (Vivaldi World Limited), 85B Hebron Road, Waiake Auckland 1311; Tel. (64-9) 473-8658; fax (64-9) 473-6887.

South Africa: Singapore Tourism Board, Representative Office, Marilyn Boogart (Pty) Ltd, No. 18 Reisling Crescent, Hurlington Manor, Sandton 2146, Johannesburg; Tel. (27-11) 789-6506; fax (27-11) 781-2491.

UK: Singapore Tourism Board, 1st floor, Carrington House, 126-130

Travel Tips

Regent Street, London W1R 5FE; Tel. (44-207) 437-0033, (08080) 656565; fax (44-207) 734-2191.

US: Singapore Tourism Board, Two Prudential Plaza, 180 North Stetson Avenue, Suite 2615, Chicago, IL 60601; Tel. (312) 938-1888; fax (312) 938-0086. Singapore Tourism Board, 8484 Wilshire Boulevard, Suite 510, Beverly Hills, CA 90211; Tel. (323) 852-1901; fax (323) 852-0129. Singapore Tourism Board, 590 Fifth Avenue, 12th floor, New York, NY 10036; Tel. (212) 302-4861; fax (212) 302-4801.

In **Singapore**, the Singapore Tourism Board is located at Tourism Court, 1 Orchard Spring Lane (off Orchard Road), Singapore 247729; Tel. (65) 6736-6622; fax (65) 6736-9423.

There is a 24-hour tourist information hotline (toll-free in Singapore only): Tel. 1800-736-2000.

Convenient Singapore Visitor Information Centres are located at Tourism Court, 1 Orchard Spring Lane (Monday to Friday 8:30am to 5pm, Saturday 8:30am to 1pm) and Suntec City Mall (#01-35), 3 Temasek Boulevard (daily 8am to 8:30pm).

W

WATER

Tap water is perfectly safe to drink in Singapore. Bottled water (local and international brands) is widely available for purchase.

WEB SITES

The Internet provides many sites for information about Singapore. It is possible to book flights and accommodations online as well.

<www.changi.airport.com.sg> Changi Airport
<www.stayinsingapore.com> Hotel (on-line bookings)
<www.nhb.gov.sg> Museums (national)
<www.singaporeair.com> Singapore Airlines

Singapore

<*www.newasia-singapore.com*> and <*www.stb.com.sg*> Singapore Tourism Board (STB)
<*www.asia1.com.sg/straitstimes*> *Straits Times* newspaper

WEIGHTS and MEASURES

Length

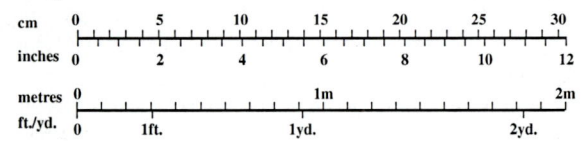

Weight

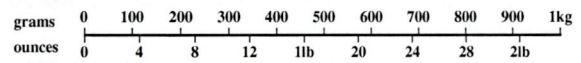

Temperature

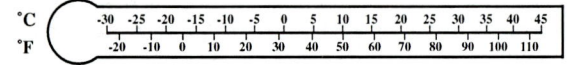

Y

YOUTH HOSTELS

Singapore has no youth hostels, but some inexpensive "backpacker" inns offer dormitories and small rooms with shared baths. The Singapore Tourism Board's free brochure, *Budget Hotels*, lists dozens of economical lodgings in four price categories, starting at under SGD39, with descriptions and complete contact information. A favorite of backpackers is the 25-room Waterloo Hostel at 55 Waterloo Street on the fourth floor of the Catholic Welfare Centre in the Civic District (Tel. 6336-6555; fax 6336-2160; <www.waterloohostel.com.sg>, which offers clean, inexpensive lodgings with the choice between dormitories and private rooms with bath.

Recommended Hotels

Recommended Hotels

Singapore has several of the world's top-rated luxury hotels, a number of new boutique hotels, and some of the cleanest budget rooms in Asia.

Posted hotel prices tend to be fairly expensive, but hefty discounts are common. Occupancy is at its highest during the high season (August and December to the end of Chinese New Year) and reservations are recommended. You can book a room yourself on the Singapore Hotel Association's web site (<www.staysinsingapore.com>), which includes full descriptions, rates, and specials for nearly every hotel and inn in Singapore.

All accommodations take major credit cards, except where noted. Meals are normally not included, although some hotels and resorts have package specials that include buffet breakfasts.

Each entry is marked with a symbol indicating the approximate room rate charged, per night, for a double room with bath. Prices do not include the 10% service charge, 3% goods and services tax, and 1% government entertainment tax, except where noted.

$	up to SGD80
$$	SDG80–200
$$$	SDG200–350
$$$$	SDG350–500
$$$$$	SDG500 and more

Berjaya Hotel $$$ *83 Duxton Road, Singapore 089540; Tel. 6227-7678; fax 6227-1232. Web site <www.berjayaresorts.com>.* Chinatown's most elegant boutique hotel, the Duxton decorates its rooms with colonial and Straits Chinese furnishings. 49 rooms.

Singapore

Conrad Centennial Singapore $$$$ *2 Temasek Boulevard, Singapore 038982; Tel. 6334-8888; fax 6333-9166. Web site <www.conradhotels.com>.* Geared to upscale business travelers, this 1997 luxury Hilton provides large rooms and top services. Disabled access. 509 rooms.

Fort Canning Lodge YWCA $$ *6 Fort Canning Road, Singapore 179494; Tel. 6338-4222; fax 6337-4222. Web site <www.ywcafclodge.org.sg>.* Recently renovated and in a quiet neighborhood, the YWCA has dorms and rooms, some with private baths, for single women, couples, and families. 212 rooms.

Four Seasons $$$$$ *190 Orchard Road, Singapore 248646; Tel. 6734-1110; fax 6733-0682. Web site <www.fourseasons.com/singapore>.* Built to compete with Asia's most upscale hotels, the elegant Four Seasons has a prime location and a vast fitness and recreation center. Disabled access. 254 rooms.

The Fullerton $$$$$ *1 Fullerton Square, Singapore 049178; Tel. 6733-8388; fax 6735-8388. Web site <www.fullertonhotel.com>.* Created within a 1928 colonial landmark fronting Marina Bay, the Fullerton is aiming to become Asia's top upscale hotel, with grand facilities and services to match. Disabled access. 400 rooms.

The Gallery Hotel $$$–$$$$ *76 Robertson Quay, Singapore 238254; Tel. 6846-8686; fax 6836-6666.* Singapore's most stylish boutique hotel brings high-tech style to its compact rooms. Breakfast over the Singapore River includes unlimited free Internet access. Disabled access. 222 rooms.

Goodwood Park $$$$ *22 Scotts Road, Singapore 228221; Tel. 6737-7411; fax 6732-8558. Web site <www.goodwoodparkhotel.com.sg>.* A National Landmark, dating from 1900, this grand hotel in expansive gardens off Orchard Road is renowned for its service, dining, and romantic interiors. 235 rooms.

Recommended Hotels

Grand Copthorne Waterfront $$$ *392 Havelock Road, Singapore 169663; Tel. 6733-0880; fax 6737-8880. E-mail <grand-copthorne@cdlhotels.com.sg>*. Luxury hotel located right on the Singapore River, the Grand Copthorne has a marvelous riverside ambience and al fresco dining. Disabled access. 537 rooms.

Grand Hyatt $$$$$ *10 Scotts Road, Singapore 228211; Tel. 6738-1234; fax 6732-1696. Web site <www.singapore.hyatt.com>*. A top luxury hotel, for over three decades, the Hyatt has turned half its rooms into large business suites for business travelers. Disabled access. 693 rooms.

Grand Plaza $$$–$$$$ *10 Coleman Street, Singapore 179809; Tel. 6336-3456; fax 6339-9311. Web site <www.plazapacifichotels.com>*. Located in the historic Civic District, this luxury hotel has an excellent spa. Disabled access. 330 rooms.

Hilton International $$$$ *581 Orchard Road, Singapore 238883; Tel. 6737-2233; fax 6732-2917. Web site <www.hilton.com>*. Since 1970, the Hilton has been a favorite of international business travelers for its central location, rooftop pool, and good dining. Disabled access. 423 rooms.

Holiday Inn Park View Singapore $$$ *11 Cavenagh Road, Singapore 229616; Tel. 6733-8333 or (800) 465-4329; fax 6734-4593. Web site <www.holidayinn.com.sg>*. North of Orchard Road near Istana, this Holiday Inn has clean, modern rooms, an efficient staff, and a top-rated Indian restaurant. Disabled access. 310 rooms.

Hotel 81 – Opera $ *238 Joo Chiat Road, Singapore 427495; Tel. 6344-8181 or 6748-8181; fax 6342-0991. Web site <www.hotel81.com.sg>*. There are nearly a dozen of these clean and comfortable budget hotels in the colorful Geylang and Joo Chiat neighborhoods, within walking distance of bus stops and MRT stations. Compact rooms have private baths, TVs, phones. Disabled access. 84 rooms.

Singapore

Hotel New Otani Singapore $$$ *177A River Valley Road, Singapore 179031; Tel. 6338-3333 or (800) 421-8797; fax 6339-2854. Web site <www.newotani.com>.* Perched on Clarke Quay, the New Otani has modern rooms with balconies and offers organized walking tours and free Singapore River cruises. 408 rooms.

Inter-Continental $$$$ *80 Middle Road, Singapore 188966; Tel. 6338-7600; fax 6338-7366. Web site <www.singaporeinterconti.com>.* Built over Bugis Street, this award-winning luxury tower offers shophouse theme rooms with Peranakan artifacts. Disabled access. 406 rooms.

Mandarin Singapore $$$$ *333 Orchard Road, Singapore 238867; Tel. 6737-4411; fax 6732-2361. Web site <www.mandarin-singapore.com>.* This towering luxury hotel, recently renovated, is topped by Singapore's highest revolving restaurant. 1,200 rooms.

Marriott $$$$ *320 Orchard Road, Singapore 238865; Tel. 6735-5800; fax 673. -9800. Web site <www.marriotthotels.com>.* Located right at the corner of Orchard and Scotts Roads, this Marriott has spacious rooms and a contemporary Chinese décor inside and out. Disabled access. 373 rooms.

Metropole $$ *41 Seah Street, Singapore 188396; Tel. 6336-3611; fax 6339-3610. Web site <www.metrohotel.com>.* A good mid-range hotel, next to the Raffles Hotel, the no-frills Metropole offers clean, modern rooms and free continental breakfast. 54 rooms.

Pan-Pacific $$$$ *7 Raffles Boulevard, Singapore 039595; Tel. 6336-8111; fax 6339-1861. Web site <www.singapore.panpac.com>.* Marina Square's least expensive, most spacious modern hotel is quite luxurious, with spectacular views of the harbor. 784 rooms.

Phoenix $$ *277 Orchard Road, Singapore 238858; Tel. 6737-8666; fax 6732-2024. Web site <www.hotelphoenixsingapore.com>.* Excellent value for its fantastic location on Orchard Road. Next door

Recommended Hotels

to the Somerset MRT station. All rooms have personal computers with email and internet access. Coffee house, lobby lounge and pastry shop. 392 rooms.

Raffles Hotel $$$$$ *1 Beach Road, Singapore 189673; Tel. 6337-1886; fax 6339-7650. Web site <www.raffleshotel.com>.* Since 1887, Raffles has been one of the legendary hotels of Asia. Recently restored to an all-suites hotel, this National Monument is thoroughly plush and historic, worthy of Singapore's highest room rates. Disabled access. 103 rooms.

Regalis Court $$ *64 Lloyd Road, Singapore 239113; Tel. 6734-7117; fax 6736-1651. Web site <www.regalis.com.sg>.* Several blocks south of Orchard Road, this small boutique hotel occupies a three-story colonial mansion with a Peranakan décor. 43 rooms.

Regent $$$$ *1 Cuscaden Road, Singapore 249715; Tel. 6733-8888; fax 6732-8838. Web site <www.regenthotels.com>.* Located a few blocks south of Orchard Road in the Tanglin shopping area, the Regent is a majestic modern hotel with fairly large rooms, an airy atrium, and a relaxing atmosphere. Disabled access. 441 rooms.

Ritz-Carlton Millennia $$$$ *7 Raffles Avenue, Singapore 039799; Tel. 6337-8888; fax 6337-5190. Web site <www.ritzcarlton.com>.* A luxury hotel with a view and larger than average rooms, the Ritz-Carlton's 32-story tower on Marina Centre overlooks the harbor, the city, and Millennia Walk shopping. Disabled access. 610 rooms.

Shangri-La $$$$ *22 Orange Grove Road, Singapore 258350; Tel. 6737-3644; fax 6737-3257. Web site <www.shangri-la.com>.* For more than 30 years, the Shangri-La's flagship hotel in Singapore has won numerous international awards, deservedly so given its high level of service, spacious rooms, fine dining, and commanding location on a large garden estate above Orchard Road. Disabled access. 760 rooms.

Singapore

Shangri-La's Rasa Sentosa Resort $$$–$$$$ *101 Siloso Road, Sentosa, Singapore 098970; Tel. 6275-0100; fax 6275-0355. Web site <www.shangri-la.com>.* Located on Sentosa Island, Singapore's top resort hotel offers a free downtown shuttle bus service, a fine buffet breakfast, free watersports equipment, and more. Most rooms have balconies overlooking the white sand beach and the world's busiest harbor. Disabled access. 459 rooms.

Sheraton Towers $$$$ *39 Scotts Road, Singapore 228230; Tel. 6737-6888; fax 6737-1072. Web site <www.sheraton.com/towerssingapore>.* With butlers for all rooms and amenities galore, this is one of the most luxurious Sheratons in the world. 413 rooms.

Swissôtel The Stamford $$$$ *2 Stamford Road, Singapore 178882; Tel. 6338-8585; fax 6338-2862. Web site <www.raffles.com>.* Until recently the world's tallest hotel, this is still Singapore's largest. The adjacent Raffles The Plaza adds 769 equally fine rooms to the complex. Major renovations recently completed. Disabled access. 1,200 rooms.

Traders Hotel Singapore $$$ *1A Cuscaden Road, Singapore 249716; Tel. 6738-2222 or (800) 942-5050; fax 6831-4314. Web site <www.shangri-la.com>.* Sister hotel to the upscale Shangri-La, Traders is both luxurious and practical, with excellent services and rooms, self-service laundry facilities, a refrigerator, large swimming pool, and a skywalk to a shopping mall, grocery, and food court on Tanglin, all at affordable rates. Disabled access. 547 rooms.

YMCA International House $$ *1 Orchard Road, Singapore 238824; Tel. 6336-6000; fax 6337-3140. Web site <www.ymca.org.sg>.* Singapore's most popular air-conditioned budget hotel, this Y on Orchard Road has single, twin, and family rooms, as well as less expensive dorms (called "student rooms"). Restaurant and McDonald's on premises. Complimentary breakfast. Requires advanced booking. 111 rooms.

Recommended Restaurants

Singapore, with over 20,000 restaurants, cafés, and food courts, has dining options to fit every taste and budget. The major cuisines are Chinese, Malaysian, Peranakan (a local fusion of Chinese and Malaysian), and Indian (both southern and northern), with healthy infusions of Indonesian, Thai, and other southeast Asian foods. There are also many fine American, South American, and European restaurants. Critics often hail the Asian dining in Singapore as the world's best, owing to its fresh seafood and other ingredients, its obsession with culinary matters, and its position at the intersection of Chinese, Malaysian, and Indian dining traditions. In general, wherever one eats, from hawker centers to top international hotel restaurants, the food and service are likely to be first-rate.

Each entry is marked with a symbol indicating the price range, per person, for a three-course dinner or equivalent (drinks, gratuities, and taxes are not included). Lunch in the same restaurant will be less expensive than dinner.

$	up to SGD10
$$	SGD10–20
$$$	SGD20–40
$$$$	SGD40 and more

Ah Hoi's Kitchen $$–$$$ *4th floor, Tanglin Mall, 1A Cuscaden Road, Civic District; Tel. 6738-2222.* Open daily for lunch and dinner. Ah Hoi's has superb Peranakan dishes and many local favorites, including fried black pepper *kway teow* (rice noodles) with seafood (Teochew style prawns, fish, and squid) and an unparalleled selection of flavored crabs in the shell, from chili crab to pepper crab and beyond. Casual dining at its best, with the Ah Hoi "pancake" recommended for dessert. Major credit cards.

Singapore

Alkaff Mansion $$$$ *10 Telok Blangah Green, Henderson Road; Tel. 6278-6979.* Open daily for lunch, high tea, and dinner this restored 1920s mansion set in extensive gardens is the setting for fine formal Indonesian dining, including a traditional *rijsttafel* (rice table) banquet and a Chinese/Malay/Indian buffet. Guests dress to the hilt. Major credit cards.

Aziza's $$–$$$ *#01-21 Albert Court, 180 Albert Street, Civic District; Tel. 6276-4591.* One of Singapore's top Peranakan/Malay restaurants, Aziza's serves superb dishes that run the gamut of Malaysian and Straits Chinese cuisines, all in a relaxing, colonial setting. Major credit cards.

Banana Leaf Apollo $ *56-38 Race Course Road, Little India; Tel. 6293-8682.* Open daily. The noted specialty at this famous restaurant is the fish head curry, but the other southern Indian dishes, all served up on "plates" of fresh banana leaves, are renowned (and spicy hot). No credit cards.

Blu $$$$ *24/F Shangri-La Hotel, 22 Orange Grove Road; Tel. 6730-2598.* Open Monday to Saturday for dinner, closed Sunday. With a stunning view above the west end of Orchard Road and a swank bar, Blu has become a trendy, elegant night spot to enjoy the new California fusion cuisine, excellent live jazz, international wines, and French champagne by the glass. Major credit cards.

Blue Ginger $$–$$$ *97 Tanjong Pagar Road, Chinatown; Tel. 6222-3928.* Open daily for lunch and dinner. The Nonya (Peranakan) dishes in this intimate bistro, a shophouse with colonial touches, are exquisite. *Ayam panggang* (the signature Blue Ginger dish of chicken in coconut milk) and *ikan masak assam gulai* (mackerel simmered in tamarind gravy with lemongrass) are typical, tasty entrées. The perfect place to sample fine Peranakan dishes. Major credit cards.

Recommended Restaurants

Boon Tong Kee $–$$ *399 Balestier Road, Geylang District; Tel. 6256-0138.* Open daily for lunch and dinner. This no-frills sidewalk café serves Hainanese chicken rice dishes that locals drive miles to consume. No credit cards.

Coffee Garden $$$–$$$$ *Shangri-La Hotel, 22 Orange Grove Road; Tel. 6737-3644.* Open daily. This 24-hour buffet and à la carte lobby-level restaurant with a garden view has some of the best buffets and Sunday brunches in town, with children charged less than half price. The open kitchens turn out international fare, from wood-fired pizzas and sushi to continental and fusion creations. Always open, with al fresco dining by the garden pool. Major credit cards.

Doc Cheng's $$$–$$$$ *#02–20 Raffles Hotel, 1 Beach Road; Tel. 6331-1761.* Open Monday to Friday for lunch, daily for dinner. Doc Cheng's combines all the major Asian cuisines with the latest trends from the West to produce some real surprises, such as banana shrimp pizza and ginger tiramisu. Major credit cards.

House of Mao Hunan Hot Pot $$$ *9 #01–09 Orchard Hotel Shopping Arcade, 442 Orchard Road; Tel. 6733-7667.* Open daily for lunch and dinner. The décor is half the fun: it's crammed with memorabilia from the days of China's Chairman Mao. The rest of the fun comes as you select from fresh meats, seafood, and vegetables that you then dip in your choice of three soup stocks that are kept steaming at your table by informative waiters. Major credit cards.

Imperial Herbal $$$–$$$$ *Metropole Hotel, 41 Seah Street; Tel. 6337-0491.* Open daily for lunch and dinner. This traditional Chinese restaurant has devised tasty medicinal dishes to treat whatever ails you, from the common cold to impotence, by restoring your internal yin and yang balance. Herbal doctors are on hand to prescribe some devilishly good tonics, herbs, and entrées, including a divine Eight Treasures Chicken. Major credit cards.

Singapore

J.P. Bastiani $$$–$$$$ *3A Clarke Quay, River Valley Road; Tel. 6433-0156.* Open daily for lunch and dinner. New Californian and Mediterranean cuisines, beautifully presented, are the hallmark of this stylish eatery on the river. The wine list is extensive. Major credit cards.

Kibbutz $$–$$$ *#01-04 Capital Square Three, 25 Church Street, Civic District; Tel. 6438-2221.* Open daily for lunch and dinner; closed Sunday. Good falafel at this café specializing in Middle-Eastern and Israeli fare. No credit cards.

Komala Vilas $–$$ *76-78 Serangoon Road, Little India; Tel. 6298-7810.* Open daily. Singapore's classic southern Indian vegetarian restaurant (six decades old) provides an unforgettable dining experience with its spicy rice and lentil curries served on a banana leaf, its chutneys, and its *dosai* (vegetable-stuffed crêpes). Eat with your hands; wash up at sinks on the wall. No credit cards.

Lei Garden $$$$ *#01-24 CHIJMES, 30 Victoria Street, Civic District; Tel. 6339-3822.* Open daily for lunch and dinner. One of Singapore's best Cantonese restaurants, in an exquisite formal setting, Lei Garden is renowned for its dim sum lunches and fresh seafood dishes (shark, abalone, lobster). Major credit cards.

Little India Arcade $ *48 Serangoon Road, Little India; no phone.* Open daily. At the back of this shopping arcade is Hastings Food Court, a small treasure trove for Indian curries, Malay dishes, and drawn teas. Pick a table and order from one of the counters; the dishes are served on banana leaves. No credit cards.

Mackerel Otah $ *267 Joo Chiat Road, Geylang; Tel. 6345-5542.* Open daily. One of the top spots for *otak-otak*, spicy fish (choose between prawn, salmon, fish roe, and fish head) wrapped in banana leaf, this shop with a few tables outside is as authentic as it gets. Major credit cards.

Recommended Restaurants

Nonya and Baba $–$$ *#01-05 Novena Ville, 275 Thomson Road; Tel. 6254-9703.* Open daily for lunch and dinner. Nothing pretentious about this simple café, but it is renowned as one of Singapore's very best restaurants for Peranakan cuisine, the regional mix of Chinese and Malay influences. Major credit cards.

Original Sin $$–$$$ *Jalan Merah Saga, Block 43, #01–62 Chip Bee Gardens, Holland Village District; Tel. 6475-5605.* Open Tuesday to Sunday for lunch, daily for dinner. This vegetarian restaurant specializes in Italian and Mediterranean fare, with knockout, mock-meat cannelloni and pizzas, as well as superb risotto, pasta, and salads, in a European setting. Major credit cards.

Red House Seafood $$–$$$ *Block 1204, #01–05 East Coast Parkway; Tel. 6442-3112.* Open daily for dinner. The breezy seashore along the East Coast Parkway has a dozen good seafood restaurants at the East Coast Seafood Centre; Red House is one of the best and most crowded (no reservations), offering informal outdoor seafood dining at its best and noisiest, with superb chilli crab and drunken prawns leading the pack – but anything from the sea will be cooked to your instructions. Major credit cards.

Sanur $$–$$$ *#04–17/18 Centrepoint, 179 Orchard Road; Tel. 6734-2192.* Open daily for lunch and dinner. The excellent Indonesian and Malay dishes include *tahu telur*, a towering beancurd and soy sauce omelet. This is a good place for *gado gado* and *rojak*, too. Further branches are located in Ngee Ann City (391 Orchard Road), Parco Bugis Junction (200 Victoria Street), and the basement of Suntec City (5 Temasek Boulevard). Major credit cards.

Satay Club $–$$ *Read Street, Clarke Quay; no phone.* Open daily for dinner. A score of street vendors barbecue skewers of mutton, beef, or chicken, served over rice on coconut leaves nightly on the bank of the Singapore River. The mutton soup (*sup kambing*) and fried noodles (*mamak mee goreng*) are also tasty. No credit cards.

Singapore

Sharkey's at Rasa Quay $$$–$$$$ *Shangri-La Rasa Sentosa Resort, Sentosa; Tel. 6275-0100.* Open daily for dinner. Dine under the stars on the white sand beach at Sentosa. Try Sharkey's Seafood Sensation, a wonderful plate of lobster, prawn, scallops, mussels, squid, grilled vegetables, rice, and garlic bread. Major credit cards.

The Tandoor $$$–$$$$ *Basement One, Holiday Inn Park View, 11 Cavenagh Road, Civic District; Tel. 6733-8333.* Open daily for lunch and dinner. One of the city's most highly rated Kashmiri restaurants, the Tandoor is best known for its fresh breads and oven-baked dishes, such as the lobster tandoori. Major credit cards.

Top of the M $$$$ *39th Floor, Mandarin Hotel, 333 Orchard Road; Tel. 6737-4411.* Open daily for lunch and dinner. One of Singapore's most romantic dinner venues, this revolving restaurant offers continental choices prepared by French chefs. The view is magnificent but prices are high. Major credit cards.

Town Restaurant and Bar $$$$ *1 Fullerton Square, Fullerton Hotel, Civic District; Tel. 6733-8388.* Open daily. With windows on the river at historic Cavenagh Bridge, the upscale Town restaurant, off the Fullerton lobby, specializes in fine Mediterranean dishes. Guests can also wine and dine alfresco. Major credit cards.

Violet Oon's Kitchen $$–$$$ *11 Bukit Pasoh Road, Chinatown; Tel. 6226-3225.* Open daily for lunch and dinner. Violet Oon is Singapore's best-known food writer and TV cook. The menu has set meals and plenty of Nonya (Peranakan) dishes such as *popiah* (prawn spring rolls), *laksa* (spicy noodle soup), and *bo-bo cha-cha* (crushed ice with syrup). Major credit cards.

Zam Zam $–$$ *699 North Bridge Road, Arab Street District; Tel. 6298-7011.* Open daily for lunch and dinner. For nearly a century this small Islamic restaurant has been serving superb *murtabak* pancakes with a variety of vegetarian and meat fillings. Major credit cards.